THE CONNECTED CHURCH

Four Winning Ingredients to Help Churches Engage Their Communities

Dr. Ken Thomas and Gabe Norris

Copyright © 2026 by **Connect Ministries**

All rights reserved. No part of this publication may be reproduced, distributed, or transmitted in any form or by any means, without prior written permission.

Scripture quotations marked (NIV) are taken from the Holy Bible, New International Version®, NIV®. Copyright © 1973, 1978, 1984, 2011 by Biblica, Inc.™ Used by permission of Zondervan. All rights reserved worldwide. www.zondervan.com. The "NIV" and "New International Version" are trademarks registered in the United States Patent and Trademark Office by Biblica, Inc.™

Scripture quotations marked (NKJV) are taken from the New King James Version®. Copyright © 1982 by Thomas Nelson, Inc. Used by permission. All rights reserved.

Sermon To Book
www.sermontobook.com

The Connected Church / Ken Thomas and Gabe Norris
ISBN-13: 978-1-960236-30-2

ENDORSEMENTS FOR AUTHORS KEN THOMAS AND GABE NORRIS, AND *THE CONNECTED CHURCH*

I'm happy to recommend *The Connected Church* by my friends Gabe Norris and Ken Thomas! I have deep respect for these brothers. Some of my earliest ministry experiences involve stories with these passionate servants of Christ. They have a contagious passion for reaching people with the gospel, and a tremendous skill for creating remarkable experiences that attempt to do this urgent work. In this great book, they share proven strategies for churches to get "unstuck" in their outreach endeavors, helping them attract new people authentically and to engage their context effectively.
Dr. Tony Merida, Pastor of Imago Dei Church, NAMB Send Network Vice President of Planter Development

At Trilith, we set the stage and enrich the lives of storymakers who inspire the world. As such, we're more than just our world-class studio lot. We understand storymakers don't just need a stage; they need a home to feel cared for, to connect, to live. In a similar way, people visiting churches are also looking for something more as they seek the love of God and the hope of the gospel. They, too, need connection, community and a sense of belonging. With this book, Ken Thomas and Gabe Norris come alongside church leaders and laypeople to share what they've learned over many years of helping ministries attract, retain, and meet the needs of their neighbors in enduring, relevant and meaningful ways. Together, Ken and Gabe provide a clear, concise, and actionable roadmap for churches

eager to better serve newcomers, current parishioners, and their local communities.
Dan Cathy, Founder and Chief Visionary, Trilith

As a coach, I've always believed that great teams are built by leaders who care deeply about people. *The Connected Church* gives pastors and church leaders a practical, Christ-centered game plan for effectively reaching new people and helping them belong—one that raises the chances of their church winning in the ways that matter most.
Mark Richt, Former College Head Coach and member of the College Football Hall of Fame

Bethlehem Church has been partnering with Connect Ministries for years—from hosting Connect Camps summer programs for our elementary schoolers, to attending and speaking at Connect Conferences. From our experience, the Connect Ministries team leads with care, intentionality, creativity, and excellence, and they are steadfast in their mission to make the gospel known. I believe this book is a great tool for showing churches how to do the same in their communities.
Jason Britt, Lead Pastor, Bethlehem Church, Winder, GA

The Connected Church is essential for anyone in ministry. Ken Thomas and Gabe Norris have worked with hundreds of churches, and they give godly wisdom to help churches connect with their community. In an age where churches are dying, this book will help grow your church or ministry. Don't miss this book. Buy it, read it, and apply it today.
Jeff Simmons, Senior Pastor and Founder of Rolling Hills Community Church

In a time when many churches are struggling to connect with their communities, Ken Thomas and Gabe Norris offer an actionable and deeply spiritual guide in *The Connected Church*.

With wisdom forged from decades of ministry and a heart for the local church, they present a compelling vision for how churches can become places of remarkable experiences, authentic relationships, and strategic impact. Every pastor, ministry leader, and church team should read it, reflect on it, and implement its insights. It's a game-changer for churches ready to grow in both depth and reach.
John W. White, III, Co-founder of Impact 360 Institute

At FCA, our mission is to lead every coach and athlete into a growing relationship with Jesus Christ and His church. As fellow ministers of the Gospel, we know that mission is getting harder and harder. In order to make meaningful connections in today's ministry climate, a good game plan is needed. *The Connected Church* does just that. This book lays out a plan to foster growth and engagement and increase spiritual vitality through the use of their Four Key Ingredient recipe: Remarkable Experiences, Life-Giving Relationships, a Clear Plan, and a Deep Friendship with God. Paired with the idea of the Remarkable Wheel, which gives seven key parts to maintain ministry momentum, *The Connected Church* provides churches with what they need to have authentic connection and vibrant ministry. What FCA seeks to provide for coaches and athletes through our E3 Discipleship Strategy of Engage, Equip, and Empower, *The Connected Church* provides for churches in this helpful resource.
Shane Williamson, President and CEO of Fellowship of Christian Athletes

In a time when many churches are struggling to connect with their communities, this book offers both a lifeline and a roadmap. With wisdom forged through real-life experience, clarity, warmth, and hard-won insight, Gabe Norris and Ken Thomas lay out practical, actionable steps to shift from stagnation to momentum—meeting people where they are, loving them remarkably well, and welcoming them into life-

changing encounters with Jesus. Reading this book feels like sitting down with trusted guides who know the terrain of church life inside and out—and are cheering you on every step of the way. The recipe works, and it's about to get really fun.
Mandy Arioto, President and CEO of MomCo Global

The Connected Church is a bridge connecting the church and the unchurched through practical and biblically-grounded methods that develop authentic relationships and lasting transformation. With insights developed through proven methods across various cultures and communities, this work shows how to make the Gospel both accessible and deeply relevant to those not seeking it. Every pastor, ministry leader, and believer who longs to fulfill the Great Commission should add this to their library and read it with a heart ready to act.
Dr. Robert Smith, Jr., Distinguished Professor of Divinity, Beeson Divinity School

This book is for every pastor who has ever looked out at a sanctuary full of faithful regulars and silently wondered, *Where are all the new families?* Every church leader needs this book. Read it with your team. Talk about it in your staff meetings. Let it reshape the way you think about connection with your community. Because, as Ken and Gabe remind us, the recipe really does matter. And here's the best part: this isn't about growing attendance. It's about faithfully stewarding the mission Jesus gave us to meet people, love them well, and help them grow closer to Him.
Les Bradford, CEO and Co-founder of YM360

I've known Gabe Norris and Ken Thomas for over thirty years. Each time I get the chance be around them, I leave looking forward to the next time we can get together. The future of every church is directly related to its desire and passion to connect with its community. In their new book, *The Connected Church*, Ken Thomas and Gabe Norris provide the recipe for

this to happen. It's the same recipe that they have used to create their remarkable organization called Connect Ministries and one that I have seen play out in their lives for [decades] now. Thankfully, now we all can learn and put into practice what we have experienced in and through their lives and ministry. If your church is looking to connect with new people, I wholeheartedly recommend you read and put the principles of this book into practice.
Dave Rhodes, Co-founder of Clarity House, Strategic Director for the Grace Family of Churches

As Christians drift more and more toward a posture of insulation and self-protection, churches must recover the truth that Jesus has sent His followers into the world. That outward-facing posture is what *The Connected Church* is all about. Written by two men who care deeply about Jesus, His mission, and the local church, this book will not only inspire you to look outside but also equip you with the tools to help the congregation do the same.
Dr. Michael Kelley, former Senior Vice President of LifeWay Christian Resources, Executive Director of Rooted Network

Ken and Gabe are great at a lot of things, but there are a few things they particularly excel at: they connect volunteers to their local churches, they connect churches to their communities, and they help communities move closer to Jesus. I couldn't be more excited about *The Connected Church*: their biblical, practical, replicable (and proven!) methods will be sure to help your church become a church that connects!
Danny Franks, Pastor of Guest Services and Events, The Summit Church, Durham, NC

I'm so thankful for the ministry of Gabe and Ken and their unwavering goal of serving the local church. They've taken one of the most foundational elements of every church and ministry—how to meet people and help them feel truly

connected—and challenged us to think differently about how to do it better. Thank you for letting so many ministry leaders benefit from your work with so many churches!
Diana Pendley, Minister to Children, Prestonwood Baptist Church

Gabe and Ken are incredible thinkers and developers of processes—processes that actually work! Their heart is always to help others grow and improve. I'm excited for how this book can equip churches of all sizes to be more effective for the Kingdom.
English Preston, Kids Ministry Director, East Cooper Baptist Church

Ken Thomas and Gabe Norris founded Connect Ministries to serve churches. Not simply to serve churches, but to equip them with specific strategies to reach new people in their communities. If your church needs fresh, proven approaches to its outreach efforts, this book is what you have been waiting for.
Dr. Phil Alsup, Executive Director, Impact 360 Institute

The world is filled with churches that mean well, and are even doctrinally sound, but still can't seem to reach their communities. Too often, there is a disconnect between desire and execution, between theology and practice. My friends Ken Thomas and Gabe Norris co-founded Connect Camps, a dynamic ministry that has been helping local churches connect with their communities for almost two decades. In *The Connected Church*, they share some of the insights they've learned along the way—the "ingredients" that help make up the "recipe" of a church that connects meaningfully with the lost. *The Connected Church* is full of biblical wisdom, transferrable

principles, and practical advice for pastors and other ministry leaders. Highly recommended.
Dr. Nathan Finn, Professor of Faith and Culture, Executive Director of the Institute for Faith and Culture, North Greenville University

Ken Thomas and Gabe Norris have spent almost twenty years studying and analyzing the most effective ways for churches to engage their communities and now they have put those results together for us in this incredible book! Our church has experienced their expertise first-hand as we have partnered with their ministry hosting Connect Camps to engage our local community. *The Connected Church: Four Winning Ingredients to Help Churches Engage Their Communities* is a must-read for churches longing to make a lasting impact beyond the walls of their church. It will inspire and equip the leaders with real-world strategies to engage people with love, belonging, and purpose.
Danny Downing, Associate Pastor, Sports and Fitness, Johnson Ferry Baptist Church, Marietta, GA

Driven by a passion for connecting churches to their communities, in 2006, innovators Ken Thomas and Gabe Norris transformed "camping" into a "mobile camping experience" for thousands of churches across the country to use as an outreach tool. With decades now of experience working directly with hundreds of churches, the practical ways of connecting they share in this book aren't just ideas, but proven methods that work! If you desire for your church to connect and mobilize the people all around you, don't miss out on *The Connected Church*.
Reed Livesay, CEO, Pine Cove Camps

Ken Thomas and Gabe Norris serve up a proven recipe for connecting churches and communities: remarkable experiences, life-giving relationships, a clear plan, and a deep friendship with God. They don't just share the menu—they've lived it through leading Connect Ministries and beyond. *The Connected Church* is a winning recipe for any leader hungry to impact their community and witness lives changed for eternity. **Pam Dishongh, Minister of Education and Administration, FBC, Pasadena, TX**

To all the churches, pastors, and church leaders who long to reach the lost and unchurched people with the message of Jesus Christ and are eager to learn how to effectively minister to new people every week.

To every team member who has served at Connect Ministries—you have played a major role in the creation of this content.

To Norma and Allyson for believing in the vision of Connect Ministries and for supporting us in this crazy but fun calling.

CONTENTS

Foreword by Jeff Henderson i
The Recipe Matters v
Ingredient #1— Providing Remarkable Experiences 11
The Remarkable Wheel— Turning Your Church Around 29
Ingredient #2— Build Life-Giving Relationships 71
Ingredient #3— Execute a Clear Plan 109
Ingredient #4— Enjoy Deep Friendship with God 147
Think Like a Chef 179
About the Authors 187
Notes 191

Foreword by Jeff Henderson

Why would you do this?"

It was the question we were hoping to hear. The leadership team at our church was meeting in a new doughnut shop in our community. We introduced ourselves to the owner and asked if we could feature her business on our church's Instagram page.

"How much does it cost?" she asked.

"Nothing, it's free."

After a puzzled look and a few moments' pause, she asked, "Do you want me to put flyers out about the church here in the shop?"

"No, that's kind but not necessary," we said.

After another perplexed look, she asked us why. In other words, why were we willing to help her, for free?

"Helping you is what's in it for us," I said. "A business like yours helps our community become stronger because of the jobs you provide and the support you give our local economy. When you win, we win."

Too often, we wait for the community to come to the church. But what if we made the first move? What if, for example, we regularly moved our team meetings out of the church building and into the community? What if we stopped talking all the time about what's happening in our church and started leveraging our social media to highlight what leaders and groups are doing in our community? What if, as Gabe and Ken share in their new book, we became a connecting church?

There's a reason why their organization is called Connect Ministries. They know how to connect churches, pastors, and communities together. They help churches meet new people while also understanding the demands that ministry places on your time and energy. It's why they also have a heart for helping pastors stay connected to the Lord. As a pastor, you're pushing against darkness, and please don't forget — darkness will push back. It's why you need a plan to remain inspired. Getting inspired requires a moment. Remaining inspired requires a plan. In *The Connected Church*, Gabe and Ken provide a plan for you and your team — a plan that's proven, easy to follow, and will deepen connections within and outside of your church.

Now more than ever, we need connecting churches that make profound impacts on their communities. Here's why: every week, a church closes down and a community never notices. They weren't connected. It's why this question is one for your leadership team and board to wrestle with: "If our church closed down tomorrow, would the community care? Would they feel the impact of the loss?"

And then, after discussing those questions, the next step is reading this book together. We can all get better at connecting. Gabe and Ken have a proven track record on how to do this. It's why I'm grateful they're sharing their secrets with us through *The Connected Church*.

Jeff Henderson | Author of best-selling book, *Know What You're FOR*

INTRODUCTION

The Recipe Matters

"We have not had a new family visit our church in at least six weeks." These were the actual words of a real-life pastor. He looked right into our eyes and shared this news with a heavy heart. We just sat there in silence for a moment. We all stared at each other. It was an awkward moment, for sure.

It wasn't that they were in a small town or a rural church. They were actually right in the middle of one of the largest cities in the United States. There were people everywhere. Cars were driving by their property by the thousands every single day. There are neighborhoods and shopping centers all around this part of the big city. People were literally everywhere—everywhere but in his church.

With frustration and discouragement in his voice, the pastor shared what it was like to work hard all week, only to see the same families week after week. He felt defeated and rejected. What do you say to a pastor who is working hard, loves his church family, loves Jesus, and wants to do his best for his

Savior, yet is not seeing the results he had dreamed of experiencing when he became the pastor of the church?

> *Why are some churches much more effective at meeting new people than others? Why is it that two churches that do similar programs experiences such different results?*

As we left that meeting, Gabe and I (Ken) asked ourselves, "What was he really saying to us? What question or statement is the underlying issue in his bold statement about not meeting new families?" If we could identify that, then maybe we could help other pastors in similar situations.

He was really saying, "We do not know how to meet new people. We know how to welcome them onto our property. We have greeters and such, but we don't know how to really 'meet' them in a way that they will stick around. We have done everything we can think of: created sports leagues, changed service times, found new pastors and staff, knocked on doors, switched curriculum, and altered our worship style. We have sat in rows. We have sat in circles. We have remodeled. We have recruited and trained volunteers. We have fall festivals. We have tried another church's blueprint and models—the list goes on, but meeting new families and assimilating them into our church is just not happening."

So, this begs the question: why are some churches much more effective at meeting new people than others? Why is it that two churches that do similar programs experience such different results?

Questions like these have focused our research and conversations with churches and parents for over twenty years. When we say "we," this is not just referring to Ken and Gabe—we are talking about our entire team. Many of our team members have participated in this journey to understand how we can help churches meet new people.

Connect has worked with several thousand churches and had several hundred thousand campers attend our camps over the years. We have had hundreds of face-to-face conversations with ministry leaders, pastors, church members, church attendees, and people who don't care about the church. We have done surveys and analyzed those surveys to try to understand what makes some churches effective at meeting new people while other churches seem to struggle. We have had hundreds of hours of video calls and phone calls with church staff over the years, trying to gain understanding and learn the similar patterns of church culture that might help us as we partner with churches.

What we have found over this extensive process is that four main distinctives are present in churches that are meeting new people and growing versus churches that are not meeting new people or growing. We call these distinctives our "ingredients."

Have you ever had someone cook something for you, and when you tasted it, you knew something wasn't right? You just knew—something was off. It can be kind of awkward because they cooked this special treat for you, and they are awaiting your response, but you bite into it, and it is tough to swallow.

> *Ingredients matter whether you are baking Christmas cookies or leading a church.*

Once, we had a coworker who was excited that his wife was bringing freshly baked cookies to the office. It was Christmastime, and everyone was in the Christmas spirit. Christmas music was playing, and everyone was eagerly waiting for the delicious, homemade, freshly baked ginger snap cookies to arrive. As soon as she pulled into the parking lot, everyone left the office and gathered in our small kitchen and break area. We could smell the spice, and we could not wait to dig into those cookies. One by one, we all grabbed a cookie.

With great anticipation, she waited for us to brag about those gingersnap cookies. Once we all took one bite, we realized something was off. Those cookies were so spicy, it tasted like we had put a piece of atomic candy into our mouths. Our mouths were burning like we had swallowed a match. To say the least, it was a complete disappointment. We were expecting one thing, and we got something completely different. We later learned that she had accidentally put way too much ginger in the cookie batter, which caused them to be super spicy.

Ingredients matter whether you are baking Christmas cookies or leading a church. If you get the ingredients wrong, it is impossible to get the great-tasting cookie that you thought you were baking. This is also true with the church—

if the ingredients are not right, you will not get the results you desire.

Our goal is not to sell you a curriculum, push a program, or sell a one-size-fits-all solution, but rather to give you the "ingredients" we have discovered over almost twenty years of research so that you can apply them to your church. It doesn't matter if you serve in a big or small church, contemporary or traditional, urban or rural. These ingredients, when all are applied, can help your church establish a culture where meeting new people is the expectation. If you read this book with a teachable spirit and look for ways to apply it to your situation, you will be on your way to thinking like a person and eventually like a church that meets new people on a regular basis.

We are aware that some may be quick to say, "Wait, the way to reach new people is to preach the gospel or to have the newest evangelistic program." Or some might say, "You have to make sure that your church is Christ-centered and focused on global missions." We agree with that.

In fact, we wrote this book presuming your church already prioritizes being a Christ-centered, Bible-based, evangelical church striving to reach people in your community and around the world with the message of Jesus Christ. We are making the assumption that your church believes that Jesus Christ is the only answer for salvation, and through faith in Jesus Christ, one can be reunited with our heavenly Father. We are assuming that it is understood that growth only happens through the work of the Holy Spirit—that man alone cannot orchestrate church growth. All growth comes from God alone.

The "ingredients" mentioned are insufficient for your church to meet new people and introduce them to the person of Jesus Christ. However, these ingredients are extremely helpful in creating a church that God can use to spread the Good News about His Son.

One day, as we visited one of our churches that hosts Connect Camps, a church staff member told us, "Connect Ministries has helped move our church from a backyard church to a front yard church. We have totally changed our way of thinking. We went from not seeing people who drive down our street to positioning our church where we can meet our community and not 'hide' in the backyard."

What they were saying is that they had been operating with a mindset that if people wanted to come to church, they would find it, but they shifted to a mindset of getting out in the middle of the community to meet new people. The era of "unchurched" people just dropping by one day to visit the church is over.

To become this type of church is going to take work. It will not happen overnight. It is a process and an adjustment. So, with this in mind, let's turn the page and let's get the work started. Trust us—it is worth it.

CHAPTER ONE

Ingredient #1— Creating Remarkable Experiences

Today's church is not always or often known for being remarkable or for creating remarkable experiences. That is not to say it can't be! We are going to talk about how this can happen in any local church, regardless of size or budget. Most of the time, unchurched people view the church as boring and stale. In fact, when churches do not put forth the effort to create remarkable experiences, then problems like these are right around the corner.

It's vitally important for your church to meet new people and effectively plug them into the life of your church. We are convinced that one of the main ingredients for success in this area is providing *remarkable experiences*.

People love and are even drawn to exceptional experiences. Most of us have experienced something so out of the ordinary, we couldn't wait to go tell someone about it. "Trust me, you have to come see this! I can't wait to show you!" You know exactly what this is like. You've been chomping at the bit to tell someone about the experience you've had. Maybe it was a game you watched, a book you read, a purchase you made, a show you saw... You've been there. We've all been there.

But why can't we make going to church a remarkable experience?

Big or small, we all crave remarkable experiences. Look around at our culture. Everyone is looking for that remarkable experience. And when they show up at church, they want the same. When someone in your community shows up to anything your church is affiliated with, they want a remarkable experience. Of course, this doesn't mean that every experience you provide needs to be full of fireworks. But, we need to be aware of expectations.

We don't do church to please people and put on successful shows, but if we are giving God our very best in all we do, that should include how we, as a church, meet new people—how we fulfill the Great Commission, sharing the gospel and making disciples in a remarkable way.

PROBLEMS OF NOT CREATING REMARKABLE EXPERIENCES

Maybe you have never considered the idea of creating remarkable experiences in church. Many churches have some annual events that they focus on, such as Vacation Bible School, Friends Day, Easter, etc., but they often fail to concentrate on smaller events or even Sunday mornings. In the hustle and bustle of getting people in the door, keeping the service moving, and then sending people home, churches can overlook the small details. Such details can make a huge difference in bringing people back.

Each time people gather in your church, they will come away with certain impressions. In turn, they will share those with their friends. If those experiences are not remarkable, then your church will have:

No One "Remarking" About Your Church

"Word-of-mouth marketing is one of the most powerful forms of advertising, as 88 percent of consumers trust their friends' recommendations over traditional media."[1] Businesses have understood this reality, and they are always encouraging you to share via social media, or they will offer referral bonuses to encourage people to practice word-of-mouth marketing on their behalf. When people are not positively remarking about a business, it is only a matter of time before that business is no longer in operation, or at least its profits are drastically reduced. Businesses understand how important it is for the community to "remark" about what they offer.

When churches fail to create remarkable experiences, very few, if any, people will "remark" about what is happening at your church. This is a major problem, because now one of the most powerful forms of marketing is not working to your church's advantage. If people are not hearing about what is happening at your church from those they trust, they are not very likely to step foot in your church or attend anything your church offers to the community.

We have seen this firsthand with Connect Camps. Since 2007, we've provided Connect Camps to communities all over the United States. The number one marketing strategy remains word of mouth—parents remarking about their children's experiences during the week of camp. We have done social media ads, email marketing, billboards, flyers, stickers, and many other tactics. But, the most impactful marketing strategy for local churches hosting our camps is word of mouth. So, if people aren't remarking about your church, that is a good indication that what you are offering is not remarkable.

Low Perceived Value by the Community

Several years ago, my (Ken's) community announced that Costco was coming to their town. It created quite a buzz. People were talking about it on social media, the newspaper was covering the progress, people were discussing it at the ballpark—it seemed everyone was aware of this new development in the community. I would even go out of my way to drive by the location from time to time to observe the construction progress so I could report to my wife.

Why was I so excited about this new business when there were so many other places to shop? Why was the community so excited about this news? Because people believed it would add value to their lives. There was an anticipated, perceived value. And when it opened up, people were everywhere. It was packed, and it still is several years later. Why? It is adding value to their lives by offering great products while saving people money.

When churches do not offer remarkable experiences, unchurched people cannot determine what value it is adding to their lives or families. When they can't determine the value, no amount of marketing you can do will change their minds. Why would they share their time with the church when there is no perceived value?

As Christians, we know there is value. We know that there is an eternal value that is the greatest gift known to mankind. But, they do not know or believe this as unbelievers. Therefore, we have to create remarkable experiences so that they can come to know the Truth that we know.

A Low Return Rate

I (Ken) am not a very good shopper. I know I can be indecisive and slow to pull the trigger when buying something. It doesn't matter if it is a gift or something I need—I'm just not good at shopping. However, I have learned one thing about buying gifts: it is much easier to return an item to the store if I saved the receipt. If I lose the receipt, some stores will not let me return that item and get a refund. In fact, my return rate is low when I don't have a receipt.

Statistics tell us that churches have a very low return rate on first-time guests. By some accounts, as few as fourteen percent of first-time visitors return for a second visit on average.[2] One reason this is so low is that churches have failed to create remarkable experiences. How do we know this? When you encounter something remarkable, don't you try to plan a time to return? A remarkable experience at a restaurant? You go back. A remarkable experience while shopping? You go back. A remarkable experience at a theme park? You go back. A remarkable experience with a person or friend? You look for times to go back and spend time together. It is how we are wired. Likewise, if you encounter a less-than-remarkable experience, you most likely will not return.

Very Little Momentum

All sports fans love it when their team "gets on a roll." It is so fun watching the team you pull for win the games they should and the games no one thought they could win. Fans will go to the store and spend money on clothing, they will buy tickets and attend the games, and they will talk about it with their friends—it can unhealthily consume people and be all they think about. We have all seen this happen, and perhaps we have been this person, getting swallowed up in the momentum.

Momentum can be hard to start. It doesn't happen overnight, and it usually doesn't happen by accident. It can be created by continuing to create remarkable experiences over and over again. Over several decades of working with local churches, Connect Ministries has seen this dynamic happen time and time again. Churches that seem to have very little momentum begin to experience momentum after years of executing remarkable experiences.

Churches that do not make it a priority to provide remarkable experiences can't expect to gain tremendous momentum. All churches want momentum and understand how important it is to their growth and to meeting new people. But, not all churches are willing to create remarkable experiences so that momentum can be achieved.

In the following pages, we will talk about practically creating remarkable experiences. We believe the formula we will share applies to all churches, no matter the size or budget.

> *Remarkable experiences are not about the size of the budget but are about how people feel after the experience.*

PEOPLE LOVE REMARKABLE

Remarkable experiences come in all shapes and sizes. Some are robust and bigger than life. Some are more subtle and may not cost a dime, yet they are no less impactful. It's not about the price tag. Remarkable experiences are not about the size of the budget but are about how people feel after the experience. So, let's look at some examples of remarkable experiences, large and small, knowing they're all about providing people with something worth remarking on.

Just think of all the time and money families have dedicated to being a part of the remarkable experience of Disney World. When you think of "wow" experiences, Disney is likely at the top of the list: eating that cookies-and-cream ice cream sandwich while walking around the park, hearing the music no matter where you are, seeing the castle, meeting the characters. There are costumes and kingdoms everywhere! All these things contribute to that "wow" moment, because they're working together to help you forget about standing in too-long lines and spending too much money on food and souvenirs.

Just about the time you're hot, sweaty, tired, and ready to throw in the towel, here comes a parade! Suddenly, you're not too tired to lift your daughter up so she can see Belle. You don't even remember what sweat is because Peter Pan just danced with your other child. Now, there's energy for the rest of the day! But night comes, and you are tired again. Before lethargy can take over, guess what? Fireworks! Then Tinkerbell flies off a building. Wow, what a send-off! A send-off that spurs you to come back.

As a matter of fact, you leave the park thinking, "I will definitely be back." Each of those remarkable experiences leaves a mark on your memory, accompanied by the desire to come back—and maybe bring someone else. We've all experienced this. No matter the hurdles to get there, the remarkable experience draws us.

How about going to stadiums? There's nothing like that feeling when you walk into a stadium, and the marching band is playing the fight song, there are people all around, face paint is everywhere you look, the noise meter is going crazy on the jumbo screen, and the team is about to play. All the sights and sounds of a stadium contribute to a remarkable experience that draws you to come to see the game in person. There is just something about a remarkable experience.

The Ritz-Carlton hotel chain became known early on for elegance, "the finest amenities, the most attentive and polished staff," high-quality services, and "access to the finest restaurants" in their respective cities.

> But it's not just the ambiance or luxurious rooms that make this hotel chain or the overall experience of being in a Ritz hotel different. What really stands out... is their idea of meeting guests' 'unexpressed needs.... For example, employees keep their eyes and ears open and record every guest's expressed and unexpressed wish list in the notepad they carry, and then they use their instincts to surprise and delight them.[3]

At Ritz-Carlton, the goal is to create memorable experiences that will stick with you for years after you've stayed at their hotel. One review of the Ritz-Carlton stated, "The employees don't run around asking what they should be doing next but are fully empowered to create unique, memorable, and personal experiences for their guests through their own ideas."

A remarkable experience doesn't necessarily have to be an expensive one.

I (Ken) have stayed at a Ritz-Carlton—which doesn't happen very often, I admit—and experienced this type of service for myself. One afternoon, I went for a run without telling anyone. It was a warm four-mile run, and I sweated pretty hard. A bellhop understanding what the temperature was like outside saw an opportunity to create a remarkable experience. Upon my return to the hotel, the bellhop met me in the road with a hand towel and a cold bottle of water. The young man had his eyes open, saw a need, and met it. That cost the Ritz almost nothing, but it was such a remarkable experience that I am still talking about it twenty years later!

A remarkable experience doesn't necessarily have to be an expensive one. That Ritz employee created what authors Chip and Dan Heath would call a "peak moment." In the *Power of Moments*, they point out that "moments matter. The 'occasionally remarkable' moments shouldn't be left to chance! They should be planned for, invested in."[4]

All the bellhop needed was a towel, a cold bottle of water, and the ability to see the opportunity to meet a need. I know I will never forget the way I benefited because that employee took the opportunity, as small as it may have seemed, to do something remarkable. That remarkable experience would draw me back to the Ritz Carlton if I ever have the occasion to be there again. Remarkable experiences are worth the effort.

No one wants to spend money and time going to something that's less than remarkable. But, most of us are willing to go out of our way for a remarkable experience. In the recent past, people from all over the country traveled to New

York City just to be a part of seeing the show *Hamilton*, and that was not an inexpensive ticket. People are still willing to sacrifice to be a part of shows like this.

We'd also hazard a guess that most of you right now have some sort of smartphone in your pocket or on a charger nearby. It can be a sacrifice to have that. Why do you have that? Because you desire a remarkable experience, and smartphones certainly provide them.

We know that on a morning commute, heading into the office or wherever you're going, even though you could have had a twenty-cent cup of coffee at home, you were willing to make a sacrifice. You were willing to spend a little bit extra to have a cup of coffee that's remarkable. We are all drawn to remarkable experiences.

> *Remarkable experiences are worth the effort.*

These examples of remarkable experiences that draw us seem awfully big. But, remarkable experiences don't have to be expensive, complicated affairs. One of the first things that pops in our minds when we think of remarkable experiences is our buddy's back porch. He made the biggest, juiciest hamburger. He got just the right amount of smoke in the burger. He marinated that burger with just the right spices. He cooked that burger to just the right temperature. The smell of all this burger perfection on the grill made us so excited. We left his house and wanted to talk about that burger for the rest of the night!

Look around and see how simple a remarkable experience can be. It could be the way someone at a grocery store bags your groceries or as simple as the barista at the local coffee shop, remembering your name and fixing your coffee as you walk in the door.

Remarkable is not the same as expensive.

Why are we talking about being remarkable in a book whose purpose is to help your church? *When it comes to guests who visit your church, fewer than one-fifth of first-time guests return, while over four-fifths of second-time guests return.*[5] Providing a remarkable experience is not about putting on a show to "wow" everyone. It's about getting people to come back that second time, getting them involved in your church, and getting to see the life-change only God can bring.

Consequences of Making Excuses

So, what keeps us from creating these remarkable experiences? For many years, the church has used a list of excuses for not making every aspect of its ministry "remarkable." At times, we may have all used them. They sound like this:

- Our building is out of date.
- We do not have enough money.
- We do not have enough time.
- We do not have the right people.
- The way we are currently doing it is fine.

Many times, it is not a lack of resources but a lack of understanding of how to create remarkable experiences in every aspect of the church. Too often, church leaders have said, "That is good enough—it is just church," or, "Just ask Joe to do it. It doesn't matter if he knows how to do it—he always says yes, and we just need a warm body to get it done." This mindset is limiting local churches' ability to meet and share the gospel with new people. It is not how churches that are effectively meeting new people are thinking and acting.

There is a price to pay for embracing excuses rather than making the necessary adjustments to be remarkable. Churches that choose the path of excuses very seldom meet new people. They lose people they once had. They lose key leaders, strategic thinkers, staff members with high potential, future opportunities, and so much more. Your predictability causes some to be slightly or maybe even completely disengaged.

Shifting the Mindset

What if your church refused to think like this? What if your church was known for being remarkable in both small ways and big ways? What if your large assemblies, such as worship, prayer times, and the like, were done with careful thought and planning? What if the ministry to individuals was remarkable as well? Jesus did both. He ministered to the crowds and the individuals.

Think about John 4. Jesus took time with a Samaritan woman and talked to her about her life. In that interaction with Jesus, her life was changed, and Scripture tells us she left her time with Jesus and went back and told—or you might say, "remarked" to—many others about what had happened, and many in that town believed. It was a remarkable day for her!

So, we have established that we're all drawn to remarkable experiences, and we want to serve God and reach our communities with remarkable experiences. Identifying that is the easy part. Pulling it off is another matter.

The church is not always synonymous with remarkable. When you are doing church every week, how do you provide remarkable experiences every time on top of all the other things you're responsible for as part of your job? As a senior pastor, family pastor, worship pastor, children's pastor—whatever your position of responsibility—how in the world do you create a remarkable experience for families and not drop everything else on your "must do" list? It's a tough challenge, for sure.

Getting caught in the loop of doing the same thing every week is easy, because you can pull that off pretty easily without falling behind on any other tasks. But, running that loop over and over leads to getting stuck in a pretty tough rut in which it feels as if you are too busy to plan ahead, don't have time to communicate adequately with the whole staff, and don't see a reason to change what's being done. After all, your people are still coming to church and giving at church. But, what if you're not seeing new families?

Author and speaker Seth Godin introduced a concept in marketing called "The Purple Cow." Purple Cow is a marketing concept that states that companies must build things worth noticing right into their products or services.[6] Godin claims that a product that isn't in itself unique and somehow remarkable, like a purple cow, is unlikely to sell, no matter how well-crafted its advertising. Godin believes that creative advertising is not enough in a media landscape that has people tuning out. With people skipping ads on television and having more control over what they watch and when they watch it, Godin argues that now, more than ever, it is important to remember the importance of creating remarkable products.

He teaches the Purple Cow in a business analogy. Imagine you are driving and you pass a field full of cows. For most of us, this is a common occurrence, as you barely even notice the cows, let alone any individual cow. Then, imagine that you see a purple cow. This purple cow has immediately captured your interest. You turn to the passenger to comment on how remarkable this purple cow is. Perhaps you even stop to take pictures of the purple cow and then share it on social media. Your friends all comment on and like your social media post, as they have never seen a purple cow, either.

> *If you were to evaluate your church, would you consider it a purple cow or just another cow in the pasture? Are people remarking about your church in the community? On social media? Are they texting their friends about it?*

Average businesses are like the black and brown cows that we hardly notice. Every once in a while, one of these ordinary cows can do something out of the ordinary to briefly grab our attention, but this attention is often fleeting.

The Purple Cow is a business that does things differently. The Purple Cow is unique and remarkable. It is so different that people feel the need to tell their friends and acquaintances about it. A Purple Cow business is easy to market. It stands out. It lends itself to viral distribution.

If you were to evaluate your church, would you consider it a purple cow or just another cow in the pasture? Are people remarking about your church in the community? On social media? Are they texting their friends about it?

Take a moment to think about the importance of meeting new people and effectively plugging them into the life of your church. If that is a priority, then it may be time to realize that the lack of new families reflects the lack of the remarkable in our churches. This isn't an indictment on anyone or any particular church. We have spent so much time in so many churches that we are able to identify this struggle and hopefully help churches breathe a breath of fresh air as they climb out of that rut with fresh, remarkable energy.

Next Step

Take a few minutes and complete the Connect Assessment to gauge your churches effectiveness in Creating Remarkable Experiences.

Go to https://www.connect-ministries.com/assessment and enter the code CONNECTEDCHURCH for a free assessment.

CHAPTER TWO

The Remarkable Wheel—Turning Your Church Around

We know your church desperately wants to provide these remarkable experiences for those in the community to meet them and get them plugged into the life of the church. The big question is, how in the world do you do that?

We have traveled and spent many years meeting with many churches, and we've learned from those who effectively provide remarkable experiences. As we've diagnosed, it's not that churches don't desire to be remarkable, but church leaders are busy and pulled in so many directions that it's sometimes hard to be remarkable in the experiences created. We want to help. There are ways you can help your church consistently and effectively provide remarkable experiences.

Before we share what we've learned about remarkable experiences, we want to be clear about what we are not saying. Here are four things we are not saying:

1. We are not saying your church should compromise the gospel of Jesus Christ or the Bible to put on a flashy show. Absolutely not.

2. We are also not saying your church should become event-based. While events are part of most strategies in the local church, we're not saying that your whole program should be event-based.

3. We're not suggesting you try to be Disney or the Ritz-Carlton. They are who they are. You are who you are.

4. We are not saying you need an enormous budget to provide remarkable experiences.

Now that it's clear what we're not saying, let's get to the good stuff. We're about to share with you a formula that will help your church provide remarkable experiences in everything that you do.

We call it the Remarkable Wheel. A wheel is all about movement and momentum. The more people who push on the wheel in the same direction, the more momentum it picks up. So, the more ministries at your church that implement the Remarkable Wheel, the more results you will see. For example, if only the children's area pushes the Wheel, then the churchwide results will be limited. If multiple ministries in your church are pushing the Wheel, those churchwide results are likewise multiplied.

And what are those results? People are talking about your church and wanting to come back, bringing others with them. One final note: if you want to keep producing the results, you have to keep pushing the Wheel. You don't just give a little push every now and then; pushing the Wheel becomes your new normal.

We're going to explore seven "pushes" on the Remarkable Wheel. If you implement these "pushes" into the life of your church, you'll be able to provide remarkable experiences for your community.

Push One—Build the Right Team

Maybe you have seen the movie *Money Ball*. The film is based on the 2003 nonfiction book, *Moneyball: The Art of Winning an Unfair Game* by Michael Lewis.[7] The book is an account of the Oakland Athletics baseball team's 2002 season and their general manager Billy Beane's attempts to assemble a competitive team.

In the film, Beane (Brad Pitt) and assistant general manager Peter Brand (Jonah Hill), faced with the franchise's limited budget for players, build a team of undervalued talent by taking a sophisticated sabermetric approach to scouting and analyzing players. They truly moved away from the traditional way of scouting, which made other older scouts upset and very critical of their new formulas. This new approach Beane and Brand introduced was an effort to build the right team with the very limited resources compared to other Major League teams. This new strategy found great success in building the right team and led to a twenty-game-winning streak and a very competitive Oakland A's team in 2002.

Building the right team was critical to the success of the Oakland As and it is critical to creating remarkable experiences. The very first "push" on the Remarkable Wheel should be no surprise—build the right team. A team can be a full-time team of staff, a group of volunteers, or a combination of the two. What does it mean to build the right team? This is the right question to ask whether you're building a ministry team, an event team, or a church staff team.

> *When the diversity of offering meets the unity of purpose, the outlook for success is high.*

Here are four criteria for building the right team:

First, ensure that all people on your team need to have different perspectives and backgrounds. They need to be willing to dream and think differently and ask the important question, "What if?" It is important to have teammates who are not in such a hurry that they don't take time to say, "What if we did this? What if we did that?" You want people on your team who will ask, "What if?"

Second, you need people on your team who are willing to listen and say, "Hey, let's go for it." If you have a team that is committed to providing remarkable experiences, you need people who are willing to try new things. If a person is unwilling to step out and try something new, they might not be the right fit for the team. At some point, "What if?" needs to be followed by, "Let's try it!" to get and keep the Wheel moving.

Third, your team should include critical thinkers. Critical thinkers are people who can point out the practical challenges and help the team find workable solutions.

Fourth, your team needs people who are wonderful at executing a plan. Once the dreamers dream the plan and you're all on board to try it, you must have the right skills available to execute it.

If everyone on your team had the same set of skills and gifts, the Wheel would probably have trouble moving or gaining momentum. The most effective teams are those made up of people with diverse backgrounds, skills, and talents. When the diversity of offerings meets the unity of purpose, the outlook for success is high.

But what if your team is nowhere near this ideal right now? Here are some practical steps we recommend to help you get where you want to go:

1. Clarify what you mean by remarkable.
2. Create a burden for why remarkable is worth it.
3. Start small. Don't get discouraged. Stay patient. You're creating a new mindset. It takes time.
4. You may need to do fewer things to ensure what you do is remarkable. For instance, you may start with a remarkable mail-out.
5. Develop your team members to be those who are always thinking about remarkable.

Building the right team is the first movement-inducing "push" on the Remarkable Wheel.

Push Two—Create an Appropriate Timeline

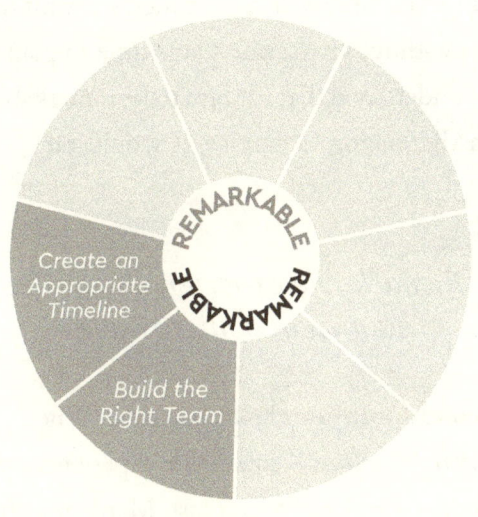

Usain Bolt will go down in history as one of the most decorated sprinters of all time. An eight-time Olympic gold medalist, Bolt is the only sprinter to win Olympic 100-meter and 200-meter titles at three consecutive Olympics (2008–2016). He gained worldwide fame for his double sprint victory in world-record times at the 2008 Beijing Olympics, which made him the first person to hold both records since fully automatic time became mandatory. When asked about his training and the dedication it took to achieve his goals, he responded, "I trained four years to run nine seconds, and people give up when they don't achieve results in two months."

Creating remarkable experiences is not something that can happen overnight. It takes time—it can't be rushed. One of the greatest enemies of creating remarkable experiences is not planning your time well. Sometimes, we want remarkable experiences without giving our teams time to plan for them. Usain Bolt understood that for him to be remarkable for nine seconds in the Beijing Olympics, it would take a four-year timeline.

> *Remarkable experiences rarely happen in a microwave.*

The second "push" on the Remarkable Wheel is to *create an appropriate timeline*. Remarkable experiences rarely happen in a microwave. They're not fast. Many of us feel like we operate in a microwave—always planning at the last minute. But, this isn't the ideal cooking time for remarkable.

It's kind of like brisket. Brisket has amazing potential to be delicious. Now, you can cook brisket in a skillet for twenty minutes, searing it to 205 degrees. Technically, it will be edible. It will be cooked. But, it won't be nearly as good as it could be, because it's not meant to be cooked that way. Brisket needs about eighteen hours of smoking to be really good. A large brisket is edible in about twenty minutes, but it's best experienced if given twelve to eighteen hours.

> *We often serve half-cooked experiences and wonder why people aren't lining up for more.*

In the church world, we run into this same principle a lot. There is often great potential for remarkable experiences to happen, but the team doesn't have time to pull them off. Maybe as a pastor, you technically preached a sermon, but it didn't really land. Or, perhaps a church event is thrown together at the last minute. You can check it off the list of things you did, but you know it just wasn't done as well as it could have been. That experience was not ready to be served. Last-minute ideas can be just the right idea, but at the wrong time. We often serve half-cooked experiences and wonder why people aren't lining up for more.

So, you need to think through the remarkable experience you want to provide. Then, work backward to establish a workable timeline. You can't be too thorough with this "push." For example, when looking at your calendar, you may realize there is too much going on for your team to appropriately provide remarkable.

One exercise your team could complete is to decide what you might say no to in the season to come so that you can say yes to the things around which you know you can provide a remarkable experience. Saying no to things is often difficult for church leaders. If this is something your church would like more help with, please reach out to us at Connect Coaching. We can help your church objectively decide what to say both yes and no to in the season to come.

When your timeline is thorough, everyone knows their roles. Everyone knows their responsibilities. Everyone has a built-in timeline about what it's going to take to pull off their end of the remarkable experience, and every part of the timeline has a due date. When you build a timeline, you're able to systematically think through the entire remarkable experience that you're planning.

> Remarkable experiences rarely happen at the last minute. They take intentionality and an appropriate timeline for you to provide remarkable service for your community. We have decades of experience training teams to create thorough timelines. Through Connect Coaching, we can train your team to build a timeline that works for you.
>
> While working with churches that have taken the Connect Assessment (which measures a church's effectiveness at meeting new people), we use a clear and concise checklist to help equip them with a practical strategy to work toward creating an appropriate timeline. Hopefully, this checklist will be helpful to you.
>
> 1. Ensure sufficient lead time. Last-minute planning isn't serving your church.
> 2. Establish role clarity. If everyone knows what is expected of them, they can each focus on doing their best in the assigned tasks.
> 3. Maintain timeline management accountability. Consider the big picture of how other planned events could impact a new event.
> 4. Determine and enforce due dates. By

establishing due dates and working toward a goal, your project will be more organized and more likely to be successful.
5. Consistently have daily or weekly checkpoints. This allows your team to share minor issues before they become mountains. It also helps with keeping you on track.

By following the checklist above, you are focused on and committed to creating an effective, remarkable experience. But remember, this is all an intentional process that requires multiple team members.

Push Three—Consider Your Resources

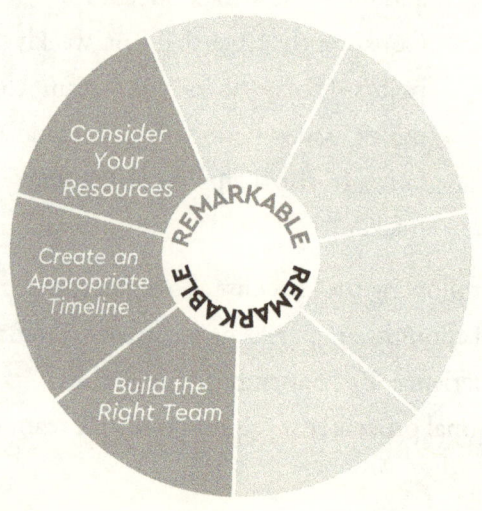

It is quite possible for church leaders to become so busy with the demands of ministry that they fail to consider the resources available to them to create remarkable experiences. Jesus was masterful at this, and while He is fully God as well as man, we humans can still learn from this example.

In John 5, we read about a crisis facing the disciples. Thousands of people were gathered to hear Jesus teach, and they were getting hungry. As the disciples searched for enough food for everyone, they found one boy who had brought five loaves of bread and two fish. Andrew brought this young boy to Jesus, and Jesus blessed the five loaves and two fish and fed over five thousand people that day. They were able to use what they had, not what they didn't have.

Be careful that you don't get so locked into what you don't have that you forget or miss what you do have to help create remarkable experiences. God can take what you have and make it more than enough if we bring it to Him.

As you strive to create remarkable experiences, you have to *consider your resources*. This is the third aspect of the Remarkable Wheel. As you implement this part of the Remarkable Wheel, let us share five specific areas to consider.

1—Talents

One resource to consider is the talents in your church and maybe in your community. It's likely some people in your community or your church are just waiting for you to say, "Would you be willing to help me with this? Would you be a part of what we're trying to do here?" People often feel uncomfortable going to a ministry leader and asking to help, but they are more than willing, and even eager, to participate when asked. Perhaps they just need a little nudge from you, asking them to use their gift to be a part of what you're doing.

2—Equipment

You also want to consider your equipment. It may not be the equipment in your one particular area. Maybe you could use things from your children's area or from the youth department. It's possible you could use equipment from other parts of the community who would be willing to partner with you in this remarkable experience. As you work together and share your equipment, you're able to provide a remarkable experience.

Also, consider the equipment you already have that might be utilized. All you might need is a dozen donuts for a visit. Maybe a pen and stationery for a note. Maybe someone in your church grows roses or loves to bake and could provide resources to help you reach out to others. Perhaps a business in your community would be willing to provide a service in exchange for a resource you could share. Pay attention to the hidden resources in your community.

3—Facility

Additionally, consider your facility and your spaces. How can you take what you have and raise it up a level? What small tweaks can you make to the space you'll be using? How can you create an environment that's inviting from the time someone steps out of their car to the time they get back in the car at the end of the experience? If you're in a room, are you considering every inch of space, even the corners? How about a parking lot or field? Whatever venue you're utilizing, be sure you use the space in the most effective way. Being a good steward of what you have includes being willing to think about all your resources, even those that might be unexpected.

4—Digital Resources

Don't forget to consider your digital resources. In today's culture, a vast majority of people considering your church will start with your social media. It often serves as an introduction to your church. Think about how you can maximize your digital resources. Is your website engaging and easy to use? Is it inviting? This is an area in which we include intentional, specific coaching through Connect Marketing which is designed for churches, some of which have taken the Connect Assessment. This isn't an area it's wise to overlook.

5—Budget

The final resource we recommend you consider is your budget. We probably all get the same sinking feeling in our stomachs when we hear the word "budget." I (Ken) remember that feeling from an experience I had as an interim Youth Minister. I had planned a wonderful event with one major mistake: I didn't consider the resources of the budget. Instead, I went way over. Way. Over. That created some very hard conversations with the church leadership.

It's important to consider your budget. That doesn't mean you need to have a big, fat budget to create something remarkable. It's great if you do, but it's not always necessary. What is necessary is that, as you think through and build your timeline, you allocate the right amount of money to make sure you can pull off the event you're planning.

Here are a couple of examples of how to be remarkable with whatever resources you have. Gabe grew up watching his father—a man who had access to some pieces of wood and a Sharpie. My father used the wood to make small crosses and wrote "Jesus Loves You" on them. He then gave these crosses out, and they had a huge impact on people. Years later, people would run into this man or his family members and remark on that cross—many still had it in their car or another place where they saw it every day.

Ken's dad, on the other hand, loved to grow roses. He would go to garage sales to buy affordable vases, or people would give him vases. He gave countless vases of roses to people who were sick, grieving, or just needed a little shot of encouragement. He was creating remarkable, memorable moments with simple roses, even if he was giving them to people he barely knew. These roses touched people's hearts and stayed in their memories.

We share those stories to say that even if you just have a Sharpie or a flower, use what you have.

You may not have access to much. But, look at what you do have and ask yourself how you can use it to provide a remarkable experience. You can be creative as you leverage your resources, whether they be facilities, equipment, budget, digital resources, or people. If your team consistently pushes this Wheel together, you may be surprised by the innovation that sparks.

Push Four—Set the Expectation Level

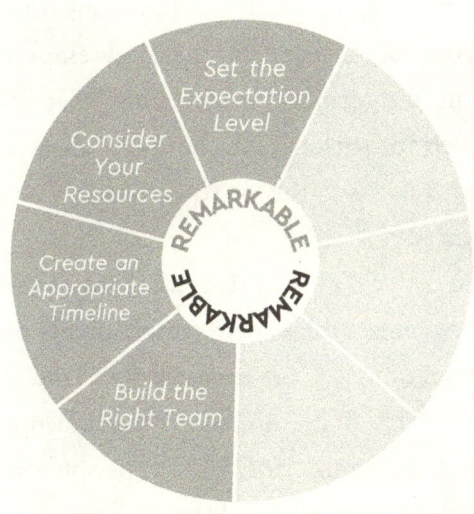

If you want to provide remarkable experiences in the context of your church, the fourth "push" of the Wheel is to *set the expectation level*. Do the people around you know what the standard is? What have you done to create an expectation level amongst all parts of your church? One of the ways that your team will effectively create and provide remarkable experiences is to ensure everybody knows what the expectation level is.

Starbucks is one company that has done an exceptional job at "setting the expectation level" for their employees. With over 300,000 employees, you may wonder, "How do they do that?" They do that with their *Green Apron Book*, a pocket-sized book that puts into words some core values that employees need to be successful at Starbucks. It offers concrete ideas on personalizing customer relationships by creating, connecting through, and elevating customer interactions. It is one of the first items that a new employee is given when joining the team. This little book that fits into the pocket of their apron clearly sets the expectations for employees so that there is no confusion regarding the way they are to treat customers.

Well, if a coffee company does this, why can't churches? With creating remarkable experiences, churches must clearly set the expectations for the ministry team and the church members. If we fail to do this, it will lead to people defining remarkable in their one terms, and one person's understanding of remarkable can be very different from someone else's understanding of remarkable.

> *When we provide remarkable experiences, we do something that's not on the script.*

Well, how do you set an expectation level so that other people are thinking like you when you're not even in the room? There are two great questions you can ask that will help those around you provide remarkable experiences, even if you're not in the planning room and even if you're not part of the execution, two questions that can help your team get on the same page:

1. *Have you created and provided an experience that exceeds the expectation of the participant?* If we're not careful, we get in a weekly rut of doing church, and then doing church, and then doing church, and doing church, and then doing church again and again and again. This often leads to experiences that are predictable to the listeners, the community we're trying to reach.

When we provide remarkable experiences, we do something that's not on the script. We do something that didn't happen last week. We do something that's not an expectation they have. It's even more than they ever expected. What could you do in the experiences you're providing that causes a family to get in their vehicle afterward and say, "Did you see what happened? Did you notice what they did? I can't wait to go share that with somebody else!"?

Some businesses are really good at this. For instance, Chick-fil-A is always figuring out what they can do to exceed customers' expectations. In the post-COVID-19 era, many restaurants simply asked customers to pardon their lack of service because of a lack of staff. Chick-fil-A changed their drive-through processes to adapt to the new normal. They turned the challenge presented by a worldwide pandemic into an opportunity to find a new way to be remarkable for their customers. This is just one example. You could look around at what you buy, where you eat, or which subscriptions you renew to find examples of businesses finding extremely creative ways to meet the needs of their customers and to market themselves to their customers.

As an example, when I (Gabe) was a young father, I had two little girls who were three and one. I walked into my local Chick-fil-A, expecting a stressful and frustrating time. How could I corral both little ones while also ordering and paying and getting the whole family to a table? A Chick-fil-A employee saw me and invited me just to sit down with my kids; they would get the order and bring my food to the table. That was huge. That was remarkable. That made me want to come back and bring others with me. At that moment, Chick-fil-A went from being a restaurant to a place of restoration. For what they did for me, I was willing to come back, tell others about it, bring my neighbors back with me, and pay full price for the meal. They exceeded my expectations, and it didn't cost them a thing.

> *God deserves our best in every area of our lives.*

Businesses can find and apply this kind of creativity to further their brand recognition, sell their product, or serve their customers. That's well and good. As churches, we have the responsibility to communicate the most important message on earth. So, why would we not seek to apply this high level of creativity and intentionality to reach those outside our walls with the love of God? God deserves our best in *every* area of our lives. Why would this be any different? We are not saying we should run our churches like businesses.

Church isn't about a big show; it's about worshiping our amazing God. What we are saying is that, as God's people communicating His word and His love, why would we not give it our all in this area of creativity? Doing the same exact thing from week to week, month to month, and year to year is not going to produce new and remarkable experiences. Why do we keep expecting that it will? Instead, we could give God our all in this area and watch His creativity pour out through us, creating remarkable experiences that draw people to our churches, but more importantly, to Him.

2. Is the remarkable experience you're creating worth talking about? Could you picture that teenager going into their cul-de-sac or to social media and talking about what you just did? Can you imagine that businessperson going into the workplace and talking about the remarkable experience that you provided? Can you picture that mom blocking out part of her schedule to go talk to other moms in her network? Is what you're providing worth talking about?

What if you had people all over town who couldn't get the remarkable experience you provided out of their minds? If you could accomplish that, you'd be well on your way to actually creating momentum around meeting new people and plugging them into the life of your church.

That's part of providing a remarkable experience. That can keep the Wheel moving. Remember, the root of the word "remarkable" is the word "remark." The experience is remarkable when people are remarking about it. The power of word of mouth is real. Whether it's the new book everyone is reading or the restaurant in town that is booked out for three weeks because everyone has heard of just how good it is, word of mouth matters. When we provide an experience that prompts people to remark positively, we are providing re-markable, and it matters.

> *Your audience has a nose, and they want to be able to smell what it is you're talking about.*

One way to make sure what you're doing is worth talking about is to communicate to all five senses. It's interesting as we travel and meet with churches and watch them try to provide remarkable experiences that they often only communicate to one or two of the five senses.

Think about how limiting that is for the participant. Think about how underwhelming that is for the participant. Every person you're communicating to has five senses. They can hear your message (you communicate into their ears). They also want to see your message. Have you given them some visual things to consider? Is there anything they can soak in visually? Have you maximized the screen available to you, the stage available to you, the walls, or the setting available to you?

Your audience has a nose, and they want to be able to smell what it is you're talking about. So, whether you're writing something or saying something or communicating something from a stage or in a video, there's a way for you to invite your audience into the message so that they can even smell the environment you're in. Your audience has a sense of taste. So, why not communicate to their sense of taste? They want to taste how good the message is. Your audience has a sense of touch. Have you given them a chance to put their hands on the content you're talking about? What are you doing to engage all five senses?

When you communicate not just to one or two senses but to all five senses, you've actually engaged the mind and heart of a listener. When you have their minds and hearts engaged, then they're much more likely to go live out the message you're encouraging them to grab hold of and take it with them. If an event communicates to all five senses and penetrates hearts and minds, it's more likely exceed the expectations of those present, and they'll be much more likely to remark about it to others. When you use these types of ideas to set your expectation level, your team is challenged and equipped to provide a much more remarkable experience.

Push Five—Provide Training

Whether someone enjoys sports, theater, music, and such, it is widely accepted that one must practice or train at their skill to be remarkable or elite. While some are born extremely gifted in a specific area, they still have to train to be the best.

Take, for example, Major League Baseball players. They are the best in the world at their sport. There are fewer than one thousand players in the major leagues. You could easily think, "Well, since they are the best, I bet they don't have to practice that much—they've already reached the top."

Well, that is not the case at all. Professional baseball players often put in several hours of practice per day. It takes training to be remarkable at anything, even for the best in the world at a particular skill.

For decades, local churches understood this important principle. In fact, in the 1960s, 70s, and 80s, churches thrived in providing local training for their leaders. Many churches had someone on their staff dedicated to training church members for ministry. Thousands of lay people would go to conferences for the sole purpose of being trained to do ministry.

Over the years, this focus on training has faded away. Lay people have become disinterested in being trained or churches have turned their focus in other directions. In many cases, churches have become teaching centers rather than training centers. Members know the gospel but do not know how to share it with their neighbors. They love their children, but they don't know how to share with them or lead them spiritually. They don't know how to be a light in a dark place. They lack the training, and because they lack the training, they choose not to volunteer for fear of failure and feeling ill-equipped to participate.

> *In our churches, we have eternity at state, and we often have the least training.*

The fifth "push" on our Remarkable Wheel is to *provide training*. Imagine you're volunteering for an event at your church or in your community, and you never get a call or a letter about training. So, you show up for the event, and someone hands you a map and instructs you to stand in a certain place and do a certain thing. Then, they leave, and you are on your own. Wouldn't you be wondering, "Okay, what am I really doing here? Do they really need me?" You likely wouldn't feel as if you were contributing to a remarkable experience.

Often, in the busyness of what we're doing in our churches, we forget that maybe those who are volunteering aren't quite as familiar with what we're trying to accomplish with a certain experience, whether that's a worship experience or something we would do during the week. It's important to remember that many volunteers may not be as familiar with our overall strategy.

That's why providing the necessary training our people need is the fifth "push" of our Wheel. Every experience requires a different depth of training. If you're doing this massive, huge event for your community, you may need to begin training three to five months in advance, using whatever tools you have available.

Depending on the event, this doesn't necessarily mean everybody has to come to the church every Monday night for three months to get trained. It may be that you use your online strategy and your social media strategy and other tools that are at your fingertips to help get your people trained. Every service opportunity, ministry, or outreach event will require a different level of training. If it's something that repeats every week, the training will probably not need to be as in-depth as it would for a big community event. But, whatever the moment is, you need to decide how much training is necessary and feasible. In that training, make sure you include the following:

Practice, Practice, Practice. It may seem simple, but it's so very important: practice, practice, practice. It's important that everyone involved is trained in their roles. You do walk-throughs, you answer questions, you make sure everyone understands their roles and responsibilities.

Provide Clarity. The most important thing about your training is clarity. Clarity on desired outcomes and available resources. An effective training is one that is crystal clear. Everyone should walk away knowing exactly what their role is and what success looks like for their position and for the church as a whole.

Clarity in training is not just about the volunteers feeling comfortable. It's about making sure everyone knows how you're going to assimilate people to the next step in the plan. Everyone needs to know the overall principle at work and how it all ties together.

To appreciate the utmost importance of this clarity, think about the places you like to go: salons, restaurants, concerts, etc. Most likely, the reason you keep coming boils down to the fact that the employees encountered there, barbers, chefs, servers, musicians, are well-trained. Those people are providing a service regarding beauty, food, or music. It's awesome that they put in the training to provide a good experience.

But in our churches, we have eternity at stake, yet we often have the least training. We can set our team members up for failure by placing them in a position and not training them. That can lead to unremarkable experiences and less volunteers and team members.

Fewer people coming to your church very well may be because your team hasn't provided remarkable.

Fewer volunteers showing up may very well be because they feel like they've been thrown to the wolves and therefore have lost confidence.

But when this is done well, when everyone is on the same page, it can be beautiful. As an example, we did camp at a church in Montgomery, Alabama, and their volunteers kept inviting campers and families to come back to the church on Sunday and the next weekend for specific events. All the volunteers knew the next steps and how to communicate them to the families who were there for camp. The message was clear, and the next step was natural for the families to take.

We've also seen the opposite happen. We had camp at a church where many campers trusted Christ. Some new believers and their families came to church the Sunday after camp, and nobody mentioned camp at all. There were no camp shirts, no celebrations of what happened at camp, no clue that camp happened at all. That's a lack of training. That's not remarkable.

Imagine if everyone on the team had been trained and ready when those new families came back to the church! Training matters. It's not just about finding enough people to show up thirty minutes early and wear a certain T-shirt. It's not just about having a certain number of hands on deck.

Whether it's Sunday morning, visits, meals, small groups, or outreach events, training is important. If we want to give God our best and do what we do for Him remarkably, then we will train and be certain everyone is clear on the goals and the steps we'll take to get there.

Push Six—Evaluate

Toyota is well known for making automobiles that you can drive for many years. One of the reasons these cars are so well built is due to the fact that Toyota emphasizes the importance of evaluation and continuous improvement. Toyota's approach is known as the "Toyota Production System" or "Lean Manufacturing." The Japanese automotive giant is renowned for its commitment to efficiency, quality, and innovation. At the heart of Toyota's success lies a culture of relentless evaluation and improvement. The company's philosophy is deeply rooted in the concept of "Kaizen," which means continuous improvement.

Another aspect of Toyota's commitment to evaluation is its use of the "Andon" system on the production line. Workers are empowered to stop the production process if they identify any defects or issues. This immediate halt triggers an evaluation of the problem, and the team collaboratively works to find a solution. This real-time evaluation and correction process have been instrumental in maintaining high quality standards.[8]

For Toyota to be successful, they embraced the concept of evaluation. It is through effective and consistent evaluation that innovation flourishes. Without evaluation, your church will have a difficult time producing remarkable experiences on a consistent basis.

> *Evaluation creates internal accountability to determine if you did what you set out to do.*

The sixth "push" on the Remarkable Wheel is to *evaluate*. Who evaluates? Everyone does. Who's responsible for evaluating? Everybody is. And when are we responsible to evaluate? All the time. Imagine the day when every area of your church was always thinking about the experience through the lens of, "How could we?" or, "What if we?" or,

"How might we?" or, "Can you imagine if we tried this?" or, "Can you imagine what would happen if we tweaked this?" Imagine the fun, creativity, innovation, and effectiveness of a team that is always tinkering, always tweaking, always dreaming, always meeting around a whiteboard, and thinking through how things could improve over time.

The initial reaction most people have to feedback is defensiveness. But, when you make feedback a normal part of your church, this initial resistance should lessen as people realize it's all about more effectively creating that remarkable experience. Evaluation creates internal accountability to determine if you did what you set out to do. It also keeps you from doing the same thing over and over again if it is not helping the church with its mission.

Practically, be sure you have an evaluation form to capture feedback from everyone who was involved in the experience—your staff, participants, and volunteers, for example. Be sure to schedule time to discuss the feedback with the team. Develop a plan to implement the feedback you decide to implement. Teach your team how to have an eye for evaluation. It's not a prompt to find things to nitpick. Rather, it is a discerning eye to see what is working, what is not working, and how you can make the experience even more remarkable.

Over time, winning teams never stop reviewing the film. A winning coach would not stop reviewing what they've done in the past and thinking through how to do it in the future.

Yet, churches stop reviewing all the time.

Many years ago, I (Ken) played high school football. In the course of my team's preparation, my fellow players and I spent several hours evaluating the film on what happened the previous Friday night. We were evaluating their performance to make changes in the upcoming week. That is the status quo for football coaches—always evaluating and planning. Imagine a winning coach saying, "I don't need to watch the film." Impossible.

If you could create a normal setting of evaluation, then you would find your church continuously improving. Who wouldn't want to be a part of a church that was always getting better, more effective, and more remarkable over time? Everybody in your church can do this; everybody on your team can do this. When you create a culture of evaluation, you're setting yourself up to more effectively meet new people and plug them into the life of your church. In our Connect Coaching sessions with churches who have taken our assessments, we provide a thorough process for evaluation.

The evaluation "push" of our Wheel actually leads to the final "push" that will help our momentum continue to build and our Wheel continue to move.

Push Seven—Innovate

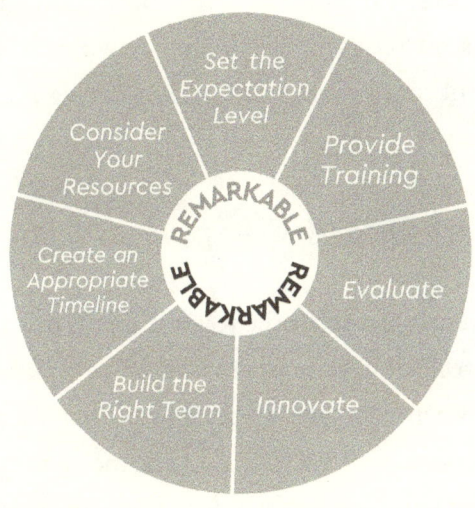

July 10, 2008, was a big day for the Apple company—it was the day they launched the App Store, which changed the game for how people interface with their smartphones. But, it wasn't just a big day for Apple; it was also a big day for Bobby Gruenewald, an Oklahoma-based pastor.

Gruenewald had been working for two years on the development of the YouVersion Bible App. Gruenewald first thought of the idea of an online Bible while in a security line at Chicago's airport in 2006. YouVersion began as a website, then transitioned to smartphones in July 2008. This app was one of only two hundred available, and the only Bible app, when Apple launched its App Store.

By the year 2021, YouVersion reached over 500 million downloads and was available in over 1,900 languages. By 2023, the team working with Gruenewald had grown to over 165 employees and over 1,000 volunteers. They now have their sights on reaching one billion downloads, and their commitment to innovation is not showing signs of slowing down.[9]

Fresh insights come from evaluation.

The seventh "push" of the Remarkable Wheel is to *innovate*. It's really interesting how all these "pushes" work together. When you provide the appropriate training your volunteers need, they understand the expectations. That allows all your volunteers to be able to evaluate, which is also a "push" of our Wheel. When all your volunteers are evaluating, it is going to lead them to this seventh "push" of the Wheel—innovation. Innovation naturally spins out of evaluation. When the culture is changing, and people understand the expectations and have been trained well, they will naturally be led to evaluate and then innovate. Since evaluation leads to innovation, if you aren't seeing new ideas or you are not innovating, it may be that you are not evaluating well.

Fresh insights come from evaluation, and that produces this innovative culture. You need people who are always asking the questions like, "How could we? How might we? How does this look if we do that?" Those questions come from an evaluative eye who's looking at a situation and saying, "I think we could do this differently." That's what you want in your volunteers as you're implementing this Remarkable Wheel.

As leaders, we can feel threatened by such evaluating questions, but we need to embrace them so we can innovate. Lean into evaluation and you just may find an innovative idea that helps your ministry or organization.

If you find your team struggling with new ideas, there are some simple ways you can start innovating.

Visit other churches or organizations: You will see people doing the same things you do, and that can validate what you are doing. Or, you may evaluate what they're doing to bring innovative ideas to your team. Innovation or validation can come out of it.

When was the last time your team visited another church or organization to learn from them? It could be a local hotel, restaurant, or website. Notice what they're doing on Instagram. Keep your eyes open for any brand that's effective in creating a remarkable experience.

We make it a practice to visit other organizations multiple times a year. This is critical to our mission at Connect Ministries. We understand that for us to continue to help churches meet new people, we must always strive to learn from other industries and organizations. We ask questions as we make these visits, like: What are they doing that would translate to our organization? What is working well for them? What can we learn from some of their pain points? How do they have their team organized? Is it efficient? Do we need to make any adjustments? How are they marketing to their audience?

Name the opportunities for growth and empower a group of people to find a solution. There is something about rallying around a common problem. Opportunities for growth can often present themselves as moments of crises or challenges. For instance, when a hurricane or tornado hits a community, we often see churches and ministries immediately working together—united people coming together to innovate, to find creative ways to help each other.

Identify needs in your community that no one else is meeting—this will help you innovate. When you see the needs, ask others how we can meet those needs. This can free you from the pressure to copycat other churches or ministries. How do you know the needs in your community? Go ask them. Keep your eyes and ears open. Go to a local school or ball field. Ask them. The community will tell you what they need if you're willing to listen. Through identifying those needs, you have a chance to innovate an effective solution.

> *Sometimes, we ask questions, and we don't take the time to listen to the answer.*

As a leader, ask good questions to those on your team. By asking good questions, you will tap into the creative minds of people in your community and church. Sometimes, we ask questions, and we don't take the time to listen to the answer. So, listen carefully and see what idea might spark in you or someone on your team.

Have a place where your team (staff and volunteers) can record ideas that need to be discussed. Ideas have a tendency to get lost because we do not write them down in a timely manner. Provide a place, either physical or digital, to write ideas down and be disciplined to review those ideas as a team. Not every idea can be implemented, and not every idea is a good idea, but never overlook someone sharing an idea, because that thought could lead to an idea that could be implemented.

When you evaluate well, you will always have a list of ideas to implement. You just have to decide which will be the most impactful. Out of evaluation comes innovation. You may feel as if you're not creative. That's okay—you can still evaluate. From that evaluation, you will get innovative ideas. Then, you just decide which is most impactful at this specific time.

For example, at Connect Ministries, in our desire to help churches meet new people, we talked to churches and realized a need to provide a remarkable experience during summer months. We knew there were a growing number of single and working parents in America. They didn't want or were not able to send their kids to an out-of-town overnight experience. This led to an innovative idea: we started doing day camps in 2007, and since then, hundreds of thousands of local campers have been impacted with the gospel of Jesus Christ.

WHEELS UP

If you'll actually implement this Remarkable Wheel, you'll be creating a tribe. You're creating a group of people who are raving fans of your church. That's what happens when you implement and spin the Remarkable Wheel, when that movement and momentum become consistent. People are bought in, and you've formed a tribe of raving fans. Your church is meeting new people, and they're plugging into the life of your church.

When all this is happening, people will go out of their way to be a part of a church that takes remarkable experiences seriously. They'll invest more of their time, they'll invest more of their energy, they'll invest more of their money, they'll invest more of their resources, and they'll also go out and tell other people.

> *Remarkable is not just a singular experience.*

That's what happens when we experience remarkable. We want other people to come with us and experience this remarkable thing. We'll come more often, and we'll bring people with us more often. Who would not want to have that at their church? This is the fruit of a team that takes providing remarkable experiences seriously.

Please understand, we're not saying that remarkable is a singular event or experience. It's not just saying, "Hey, we're going to make this experience remarkable," and then not paying attention to the rest of the experiences we're providing throughout the year.

But what we are saying is simply this: *remarkable is a culture you create.* It doesn't happen just one time. It's a culture you create over and over and over again in your community. The Wheel is always spinning—not just one time, but all the time.

So, here's the Wheel that is always spinning. Here's the key to getting those second-time guests from your community. Use this Wheel to take a fresh look at all the experiences you're providing to your church and community right now. Ask yourself, then have an honest conversation with your staff and volunteers: "How are we doing in each of these areas?" Look at each individual event you do and ask, "Do we have the right team? Are we creating a good timeline? Are we considering all the resources at our fingertips? Have we set the expectation level high? Are we providing the necessary training to make it a remarkable experience? Have we taken the time to evaluate what's going on? Are we innovating based on what we've learned through our evaluation process?" When your team is pushing this Wheel for everything your church is trying to do, you'll be well on your way to providing remarkable experiences for your community.

Consider this picture. Everything your church does is a big waffle. Remarkable is not one square of that waffle, not one part of what you do. Remarkable is the syrup. It permeates every square of your waffle. It flavors everything you do.

Let's finish this chapter with a church we've seen spin this wheel well and consistently. A week before camp, they printed off a card for every camper who indicated they didn't go to church anywhere and gave each card to one of our church volunteers. An older volunteer named Mr. Bill had a camper named Sammy on his card. He prayed and spent time with Sammy, as did another Connect Crew member named Kimberly, especially during dodgeball games. Eventually, at camp, Mr. Bill led Sammy to Christ. Sammy's mom and sibling were not part of another church family, so they came to that church the Sunday after camp.

Sammy saw Kimberly, and the first thing he asked was, "Where's Mr. Bill?" Notice that Sammy came to Kimberly—he recognized her because of her camp shirt, and he not only remembered Mr. Bill, but was actively looking for him, too.

The Remarkable Wheel

A year later, Sammy's mom and both her kids are still a part of that church.

A small church acted on mission, and life change happened. They did small things like making memories, slapping high fives, offering coffee to parents at drop off each morning of camp, wearing a camp shirt, and so much more. And we can honestly say, "That's remarkable." Because they were committed to creating remarkable experiences, big and small, an entire family was impacted with the gospel, and their eternity will be spent with Jesus.

Now it is time be *re-mark-able*. It's going to be worth it.

Remember, when you do:

It is going to leave a *mark* on people that has the potential to change their lives forever.

They are going to *remark* about it to other people who you'll have an opportunity to impact in the season to come.

We hope the Remarkable Wheel has given you the confidence that you are now more *able* to do it!

CHAPTER THREE

Ingredient #2— Build Life-Giving Relationships

THE TRUTH ABOUT LONELINESS

Jeanine Stewart, senior consultant with the Neuroleadership Institute, says, "Being surrounded by other human beings doesn't guarantee a sense of belonging. Belonging actually has to do with identification as a member of a group and the higher quality interactions which come from that."[10] People don't just need to be around people; they need to be around *their* people. Our brains are literally wired that way: "A recent MIT study found we crave interactions in the same region of our brains where we crave food, and another study showed we experience social exclusion in the same region of our brain where we experience physical pain."[11]

If you've ever caught yourself scrolling for hours through social media, you've tasted this craving firsthand. Smartphone design and addiction are a great example of how our desire to connect with other people drives our behavior on a daily basis: "A study published in *Frontiers in Psychology* found smartphones are compelling because they tap into fundamental needs to connect. According to the research, humans have a deep desire to monitor others and to be monitored by them—to be seen and heard and considered by others. It is this alignment with our social needs that makes smartphones especially hard to put down." [12]

People who have friends and close confidants are more satisfied with their lives and less likely to suffer from depression.[13] They're also less likely to die from all causes, including heart problems and a range of chronic diseases.[14] A recent Surgeon General report shows loneliness was associated with a twenty-nine percent increased risk of heart disease, a thirty-two percent increased risk of stroke and a fifty percent increased risk of developing dementia for older adults.[15]

A review of thirty-eight studies found that adult friendships, especially high-quality ones that provide social support and companionship, significantly predict well-being and can protect against mental health issues such as depression and anxiety—and those benefits persist across the lifespan.[16] People with no friends or poor-quality friendships are twice as likely to die prematurely, according to Holt-Lunstad's meta-analysis of more than 308,000 people—a risk factor even greater than the effects of smoking twenty cigarettes per day.[17]

Despite the risks, Americans are getting lonelier. In 2021, twelve percent of U. S. adults said they did not have any close friends, up from three percent in 1990.[18] That decline began well before the COVID-19 pandemic, with companionship and social engagement among friends, family, and others decreasing steadily over the past two decades.[19] An international study of high school students found that between 2012 and 2018, school loneliness increased in thirty-six of thirty-seven countries.[20]

Research by the Center for Inclusion and Belonging at the American Immigration Council indicated that most Americans feel a sense of "non-belonging" in one or more aspects of their life. According to their study, about sixty-four percent of Americans feel non-belonging in the workplace, sixty-eight percent in the country, and seventy-four percent in their town or city.[21]

The COVID-19 pandemic likely exacerbated an existing trend toward social isolation, and it also provided a natural way for scientists to measure the effects of that shift. Bagwell and psychologist Karen Kochel, PhD, of the University of Richmond, found that college students with less social support from their friends during the first year of the pandemic also had more problems with anxiety, depression, and academic adjustment.[22]

There is a lot of heartache behind those numbers. Where does the church fit in? We should be the most hospitable, personal, and most conducive environment in our towns for building Christ-centered, life-giving relationships that create ongoing and meaningful community. And if we're paying attention to the community around us, we'll notice that many people are not coming to the church to find the relationships they are looking for.

> *People are looking for deeply personal experiences.*

Do you see what is at stake for churches who fail to create a culture of life-giving relationships? If this is not a high priority for your team and if your church is not consistently effective at building life-giving relationships with people, then you should expect that:

The new people you long to meet will look for community somewhere else. And if they are fortunate enough to find some form of it, it'll most likely be in their neighborhood, with their work team, during their children's activities, at the gym, in a local bar, online, or at the dog park. As unthinkable as it is that people would find more life-giving relationships in places like these than in the church, it happens all the time.

New people will feel like a complete outsider at your church. Who do you know that actually enjoys that feeling? If you've ever been the only person at a party, function, gathering, holiday get-together, event, or meeting that doesn't sense connection with any other person in the setting, then you know exactly what it's like. Chances are if you ever returned,

Build Life-Giving Relationships

it was likely more out of complete obligation than personal choice.

> *Volunteers don't want to be recruited and begged. Instead, they are inspired to give their time, talent, and energy to places where they feel known, seen, heard, and valued.*

You'll constantly struggle to find the volunteers you need. Most churches we meet with, both big and small, live in the constant tension of trying to figure out how in the world to find the right number of volunteers they need to rightly execute their ongoing plan. The fact is, you'll always be limited in the amount you can accomplish if you fail to have the leaders and volunteers around you. Volunteers don't want to be recruited and begged. Instead, they are inspired to give their time, talent, and energy to places where they feel known, seen, heard, and valued. Many churches are bypassing relationships and replacing them with volunteer recruitment. New people can see right through it. When you don't actually know people, they'll be far less likely to volunteer. Even worse, in many cases, it will be because they never received a personal invitation to help in the first place.

Church leaders will be expected to accomplish the impossible task of knowing everyone. That's just simply not sustainable—not if you want to grow. People are looking for deeply personal experiences. In the words of Carey Nieuwhof,

"It is vital to figure out how to care for people personally—to know their names, to care about them as people. ... No one wants to be a number. In the future, treating people like numbers will get you declining numbers and not much more. The goal is not to have a church where everyone knows everybody—that doesn't scale. The point is to have a church where everyone is known."[23]

And that will never happen as long as only a small pocket of people feel responsible to build the relationships.

Your church will consist of more consumers than contributors. When people visit your church and don't feel a sense of connection, then the only options they have remaining are to consume a bunch of information, become critics of that information, or leave. That's not what you signed up for. You long for something so much deeper than people just showing up only to leave as quickly as they can after it's over. God didn't assign you to your church simply to be a content provider who constantly downloads thoughts onto listeners. If that were the case, people could just consume content 24/7 from any device every day of the week for free. You're not looking for consumers, you're looking for contributors, and contributors don't contribute to places they don't feel they belong.

People Are Looking for *Their* People

I (Gabe) was sure I would never forget the moment I sat down with my first ever college advisor. I had recently made the transition from feeling like I was a large fish in a relatively small pond. Entering a large university swiftly made me feel like a tiny minnow in a giant blue ocean.

Have you ever felt that way? For me, that deep and loud awareness of feeling small and alone was immediately heightened when the advisor immediately asked, "What is your social security number, sir?" He didn't greet me, shake my hand, or ask my name. I felt alone—all by myself even in the presence of another person, who had led with the impression I was a number first and a human second. In that season, a longing grew in me to do something far more than just find people. I wanted to find *my* people.

Do you know that feeling? The feeling of lostness when you have no idea where *your* people are? The feeling of comfort and relief when *your* people have indeed been found? If you're like us, those experiences have been some of the most deeply impactful ones of your entire life. You know it when you've found your people, and you almost can't get it out of your head when you've not. It was felt when we all entered a brand-new grade, moved to a new town, started a new job, dated someone who may or may not have become your spouse, and the list goes on.

> *The innate desire to belong is one of the most influential forces in all of human behavior.*

The great theologians Drew Holcomb and the Neighbors sing about how "you gotta find your people" to discover yourself.[24] The people you want to reach feel this anytime they are around your church. They are not seeking a great preacher as much as you might think they are. After all, they can listen to endless sermons and messages at their fingertips at any moment on any device anywhere in the world. They are not primarily seeking programs, even ones as great as the ones you're promoting at this current moment. What they long for more than anything, even if they never admit it to you, is people—*their* people—people they can eventually call their own. They want to find their people!

The innate desire to belong is one of the most influential forces in all of human behavior. Remember how powerful that craving was at recess when we were kids in elementary school? Few things compare to that feeling of knowing that you got picked by the self-proclaimed captain to be on the pick-up team. Then, eventually, we graduated from recess and moved toward many other forms of "teams." Whether it was going out of your way to see your crush at the school locker or being included in the group headed toward the local hangout spot, it felt so good to know that the others wanted you around.

It's in all of us, a craving to do just about anything to belong. The desire to belong burns so hot in people that they are even willing to participate in trending social media challenges just for the momentary satisfaction of knowing they were a part of something much larger. There are a lot of social media challenges like the ALS ice bucket challenge that dominated people's social media feeds. These types of challenges are an indication that people want to belong. Belonging is powerful, and so is not belonging.

There's no denying it—people want to belong to something, because they were created for belonging. No matter what age a person is, that desire to belong is intrinsic. We even see this with our own children. Ken's son was a sixth grader when his basketball team had a big victory on the court. He was so eager to make sure he wore a certain team-specific shirt to school the next day, demonstrating to all his classmates that he belonged to that team. Naturally, something in him wanted to show, "I'm on the team that won!"

My (Gabe) daughter loves her basketball team. You'd think she would say she can't wait to learn how to shoot and pass and dribble and do all the fundamentals of basketball, but what she really loves and looks forward to is when the team gets in a circle, with everybody focused in, and they all say, "Let's go Lynx!" Then, everyone cheers, "L-Y-N-X!"

She absolutely loves that feeling of being on the team, of being in a circle with that group of people. She looks forward to it because she loves being part of it.

Those are athletic examples, but we see this truth play out in a myriad of ways and settings. For instance, some groups get together because they have a common interest in particular types of dogs, like Golden Doodles. There are people who join groups to read and discuss works by their favorite authors, like C. S. Lewis or Leo Tolstoy. There are groups for people who like to knit, collect stamps, or garden. You can likely find a group for anything that interests you. The fact is clear: people long to belong.

Living in a small town very close to the University of Georgia, our team sees this up close and personal on many weekends during each fall. Imagine a Saturday afternoon home football game in Athens, Georgia. The stadium will be filled with members of Dawg Nation, dressed in red and black, going crazy for their team—together. Even before the game, you'll find them all tailgating together.

And let's just acknowledge, tailgating isn't cheap. According to CNN, in 2015, the average NFL fan planned to spend $196 per tailgate party.[25] Imagine you only tailgate at five games per year. That's approximately $1,000 to enjoy belonging to this tailgating community.

People want to belong so much they'll pay fees for it. Let's think about a Rotary Club. Some people value belonging to this club because they want to use their gifts to help the community and be around others who want the same. According to Rotary International, membership dues are approximately $35 every six months.[26] People also like to belong to country clubs, which can be fun places to belong. Members must value belonging, because the average fee for joining can be between $700 and $25,000, with monthly fees ranging from $70 to $1,500.[27]

It's not only physical, in-person groups that draw people these days. Many people are finding a sense of belonging on social media and in online groups. There are groups for cattle farming, classic car enthusiasts, sheepdog farmers, dancers, comedians—the list goes on. And then there are the online gaming communities: people from all over, connected through a gaming system, a headset, and the internet, can explore worlds and fight virtual enemies together. Many people will even show up to watch the best of the best play a video game. The point is, even technology is utilized by people to attempt to fill that intrinsic need to belong.

BEING WITH PEOPLE VS. BELONGING TO A GROUP

The people you daydream about reaching are the exact same way. They are eager to belong to a group that truly adds value to their lives. We know you have a deep burden to effectively engage people who are not currently a part of your local church. That's one reason we've written this book—to pour gasoline on that burning fire. One way you'll prove that you are dead serious about reaching those people is by being convinced that it is going to take more than just getting people to come to your church. Getting new people to be around people is only the starting point. Effectively meeting new people means connecting them to a group, and belonging to a group is not the same as being in the crowd.

I (Gabe) learned this firsthand at the Magic Kingdom. The good Lord blessed me with four women to live life alongside—one wife and three lovely daughters. To say that my time as a parent has been a bit girly would be an understatement.

When my first daughter, Neely, turned four years old, I did what any dad of a princess-loving daughter would do: I took her to see Cinderella's castle. She didn't need to see the castle to feel like a princess. I lost track of how many princess dresses my family had in the costume closet. She was a princess in her own mind most days in that season of her life. So, for her to actually see the castle firsthand in her very own princess dress equaled the exhilaration of a combined one thousand kids in an all-you-can-eat candy shop. I will never forget the look on her face when she saw it all with her very own eyes. The trip was surely going to be magical!

But there's one main thing I failed to consider when planning the trip—fourteen million other families were also bringing their young princesses to see the castle in person on the exact same day! I had never seen crowds so large.

Just behind the castle is the horse carousel, and by the time I had sweated through my shirt a couple of times, I felt like I was due for a freezing cold ice cream sandwich. So, my wife and I put Neely on the horse carousel, and I secretly celebrated a forty-eight-second break to enjoy my refreshing snack. Our family waved at her and screamed in celebration of every rotation of that thoroughbred horse circling about.

Finally, the ride ended, and it was time to meet my daughter at the exact spot where we had first placed her on the ride. We waited and waited. Then waited some more. The next round of riders was buckling in, and it occurred to me and my wife that we couldn't find our daughter.

My insides were telling me to be calm, but by that point, my brain and heart weren't communicating very effectively with one another. With no restraint, I screamed, "Neely!" No one seemed to look my way. I screamed louder, except this time I did so while running. Without ever discussing the plan, my wife went one direction, and I went the other. *"Neeeeeeelyyyyyyy!"* No one responded to me or seemed bothered by my problem. No one helped me. No one attempted to add volume to my voice by running with me and screaming her name. There I was, desperate to find what I was looking for, right smack dab in the middle of a huge crowd yet feeling about as lonely as I had ever felt at any moment in my life.

I eventually found my daughter (and a lot of other parenting lessons I learned the hard way). But in that huge crowd, I never found my people—people who could see me, journey with me, hear me, join me, help me, fight for me, grieve with me, and eventually celebrate a breakthrough with me.

> *If you want to meet new people, you'll need to distinguish between crowds and connection.*

Your church navigates this challenge every single week of the year. If you want to meet new people, you'll need to distinguish between crowds and connection—between being with people and actually belonging to a group of people.

We could continue to talk about all the different places in our culture where people look for belonging, but I think we can stop here and agree that people long to belong. It doesn't matter if you're introverted or extroverted or where you fall on the Enneagram. The desire to belong is innate. It's inside us. It exists. You want to belong. I want to belong. And the people you're trying to reach? They want to belong. However, as much as people want to belong, they're not going to try to belong somewhere they're not welcomed. The church should be the most welcoming and life-giving place on the planet.

You're likely reading these words right now because you help lead a church and you're trying to meet new people. We know you are. We also know people are out there in the community considering coming to your church, and one thing they're looking for is a place to belong. They want to be connected with other people. The truth is that it's not as easy as we'd like to think it is.

If first-time guests come to a church and feel like outsiders, it's highly unlikely they will somehow find a way to "get on the inside," to get connected and plugged into the life of the church. Many times, they either find themselves in draining relationships that feel as if they're sucking the life out of them or they just end up not connecting with people at all. That's a tough reality, not just for the person but for the church as well. We understand that, as a church, it's hard to create a place where people can belong.

FORMULA FOR LIFE-GIVING RELATIONSHIPS

This is where many churches find themselves. They want to spin the Remarkable Wheel and consistently meet new people and integrate them into the life of their church. But, it's a difficult challenge. So, we've cultivated knowledge from churches we've seen have success in their efforts to help people belong by building life-giving relationships. From that knowledge, and our experience, we have designed a formula you can implement to help your church build life-giving relationships.

Ask yourself this: When was the last time you went somewhere you had never been before, a place where you were completely uncomfortable? Perhaps you have experienced this when you have traveled internationally. We felt like this when we facilitated camp in an international city. We didn't know the language, how to read the signs, etc. We can vividly remember just smiling and trying to relate with people. The people were great and hospitable, but we just couldn't communicate. It felt like we didn't belong. At one point, we stood looking at a local leader as he stood looking at us. Then, we both looked at a cow. We gave him a thumbs up, and that was it. That was just about as good as we could do. This is funny, but it's not amusing when this happens in our churches.

But sadly, this can happen every Sunday at your church. People can sit through the whole service with a deep desire to belong, yet never feel as if they do. One healthy practice is to put yourself in the shoes of the people you're trying to reach.

Imagine you are a first-time guest. You've been working your job all week. You've been plugged into your kids' ballgames or working in your shop or whatever your interests are. You have a sense of confidence about what you do at home or in the workplace. This is a big moment for you, because you've decided to give this church a shot. So, you and your family got into your vehicle and drove to this church. After being confident in what you were doing all week, you now have entered into a new world with a hint of insecurity.

There's a little bit of lost confidence now. You're driving to a place you have not been and maybe you aren't even sure where to park. You finally find a spot, hope it's right, then get out and try to decipher which building you should enter. You eventually find your way into the facility, and you're surrounded by people you don't know. For the duration of the experience, not one person talks to you. You didn't know anyone's name when you came in here and it doesn't look like you'll know anyone's name when you leave. It's unlikely you'll pull a random church member aside and say, "Excuse me, I really don't feel like I belong here." Instead, you'll most likely just feel awkward and decide not to return.

Being in that situation can be alarming—it feels like the opposite of simply belonging. Why would this first-time guest come back? Nobody introduced themselves, asked them a question, or pursued them. They left the service without having any real interaction with a person. After the service or event was over, they may have gotten a generic, follow-up email they're sure was sent to a slew of other guests that day as well. Nothing personal there. The next logical question this guest might ask themselves is, "Do I and my family really desire to be a part of this local church?"

This scenario might explain why fewer than one-fifth of first-time guests actually come back to the church they visited.[28] Take a moment to wrap your mind around that last sentence. Then think about it this way: over eighty percent of first-time guests don't return to the church they visited. Now, that is something we should all pay close attention to. That's the bad news.

The good news, though, is that over four-fifths of second-time guests actually do return to a church.[29] So, the key is moving a visitor from first-time guest to second-time guest. Obviously, we believe one way you do that is by intentionally building life-giving relationships in the context of your church.

As a matter of fact, we don't just believe this; we have seen it put into practice. We've seen churches effectively meet new people, connect with those people, and assimilate those people into their church. Building life-giving relationships is a foundational part of their strategy to grow the kingdom of God through meeting new people and plugging them into the life of their church.

We have established that, in the church, it's important to build life-giving relationships, and we have seen it is possible to effectively build life-giving relationships. The next question is, "How?"

To answer that question, we have created a formula you can follow. It's kind of like algebra. Don't panic. We know algebra is challenging for most students. Unless you're naturally math-minded, algebra doesn't always make sense. The strange combination of letters and numbers and symbols written on top of and across from each other can seem like a strange language we're not sure we can learn. We can put that fear to rest, here. Our formula will make great sense.

$$\frac{G(I + C)}{T} = LGR \times \uparrow P = \text{Culture of LGR}$$

G Stands for *Go*

Going toward those you long to serve is remarkable. You know this to be true if you've ever been on the receiving end of a service provider doing the same for you. That's exactly what an eighty-nine-year-old man in southeastern Pennsylvania experienced one winter as heavy snows headed his way.[30]

We can only imagine what his daughter felt when she learned her father was low on food with a snowstorm imminent. (In our southeastern town, the locals go absolutely bonkers when even the slightest chance of snow flurries shows up on the radar. You can hardly find milk or eggs anywhere.) Understandably worried, the woman called store after store after store, pleading for someone to deliver groceries to her dad. Due to the bad weather moving into the area, nobody was able to help.

Running out of ideas, she threw a Hail Mary and called Trader Joe's. Only one problem. Trader Joe's has a company policy that they do not deliver—at least, not normally.

Given the extreme conditions her dad was facing, Trader Joe's decided to do what no other local store was willing to consider: actually go to the elderly man and meet him in his moment of need. Not only were they willing to go, but they also generously suggested additional food items to fit his low-sodium diet. As if that weren't enough, the employee informed the daughter that the cost of her order would be covered, free of charge. Under thirty minutes later, the man's groceries were delivered.

A daughter honored her dad, and a store blessed the daughter by meeting the needs of her dad. Years later the story is still being told. Maybe there was an initial price for Trader Joe's to pay for such an act of kindness, but our gut feeling was that the ripple effect impact of their intentional influence was well worth the investment.

That's the power of going. And that is the beginning of building life-giving relationships. First, *G* stands for *go*. Now, that's probably not a surprise. You might've even guessed what *G* stood for. In fact, you're probably thinking, "Our church actually talks about *go* all the time." We talk about going around the world, which is the Great Commission, and we should. We talk about going into our community, and that's good, too. We should be doing those things. We talk about reaching our state or whatever community it may be. And that is true as it relates to the Great Commission.

But as we think about this formula, let's think about *G* a little bit differently—as a mindset of *going toward people*. Think about that. Picture a Sunday morning at your church. First-time visitors show up, and the people in your church have a mindset of going toward people. They go toward the guests in the parking lot and when they come into the building. Those visitors have multiple personal greetings and invitations to belong.

When we are living with a mindset of going toward people, it goes beyond the church walls and naturally leads to engaging conversation. We go toward people at the ballpark. We go toward them when we see them in the store. We go toward them when we see them in a restaurant. We go toward the people when they come to our church.

In some cases, church staff members are great at going toward people, but the church body is not. One statistic that blew my mind and speaks directly to this issue is that eighty-two percent of visitors say that being greeted by a congregant influences their decision to stick around at that church.[31]

Going toward people requires more than seeming friendly to them. While being friendly is a great start, there is a distinction between being friendly and helping people actually belong to a group that can eventually become their friends. Churches need to do better about bridging this gap. In his book *The Power of Personal: Building Stronger Connections in a Lonely World*, Ben Mandrell says, "Being welcoming is important to church guests and potential visitors, but being friendly isn't enough. People are looking for beyond-the-surface connections. . . . Loneliness won't be solved simply by seeing someone smile once a week as we walk into a worship service. People are looking for friends, not friendliness. . ."[32]

> *It's hard to feel at home if you're being ignored.*

It makes sense. We feel more comfortable somewhere if we actually feel like the people are glad we're there. It's hard to feel at home if you're being ignored. With that in mind, why do so many church members struggle to go toward visitors at their church? Honestly, it can be easy to fall into the practical belief that the church staff are the only ones who can or should move toward people. But, the Great Commission is for all believers, not just seminary-trained pastors. When we choose not to go toward people, it leaves a big void and reveals a neglect to follow the way Jesus lived His life.

Going toward others is the rhythm of Jesus. He was always moving toward people. He moved toward a man hiding in a tree (Luke 19:1–10). He reached out to a woman living in shame (John 4:1–26). The New Testament has countless examples of Jesus healing people. And let's not forget that Jesus moved toward people when He called His disciples and invited them to join Him.

These are just a few examples. Jesus was always calling someone by name and making eye contact with them. He moved in their direction. He didn't avoid people, even if it meant He would have a hard conversation. If we seek to live like Jesus, we'll live out this concept of *Go*.

G stands for *go*. It's a mindset of going toward people.

$$\frac{G(I + C)}{T} = LGR \times \uparrow P = \text{Culture of LGR}$$

I Stands for "Take *Interest*"

Have you ever done life with someone who seemed like they were constantly thinking about themselves? What a draining experience that can be! We once worked alongside a teammate who proved time and time again that the person they were most often thinking about was . . . themself.

Remembering the times we shared together almost makes our hands so twitchy that it feels difficult to type these words. This particular teammate was fascinated by talking about themself. It was almost as if they lit up like a Christmas tree at the opportunity to talk about their own life, plans, and opinions—again. We knew just about every single thing about them: their interests, their resume, their entire life's timeline, their children's names, what they had for dinner last night, where they were headed on their next trip, what they were looking forward to, what they had invested their finances into.

Being with them was like being with a never-ending broken record. There were even times when the teammate would look at us and ask, "How did you know that about me?" We never had the guts to tell them what we were actually thinking: "We know that about you because this is the seventeenth time you've gone over this exact same chapter of your life's story with us!"

The teammate knew next to nothing about us. How could they? They had rarely ever asked us anything personal. They were way more concerned with being interesting than being interested, way more passionate about talking to us than having a conversation with us. They never showed curiosity but only wanted to share more of their own life. We are completely convinced our teammate left all our interactions deeply satisfied with how impressive they had been to us. Little did they know, the exact opposite was true. We dreaded seeing this person and felt utterly exhausted after being with them. More than anything, we had absolutely no motivation or inspiration to do anything great for them!

Sometimes, we pray for great mentors, and instead, God graces us with opportunities to be around people we never want to become like. That's what that teammate was to me (Gabe). Please don't feel sorry for me, though. I also had my grandmother, Mama Jane. Being with her was like being with a never-ending fountain of youth. She knew I loved pound cake, which team I pulled for, what I wanted to eat for supper, and what I loved to watch on television. She took an interest in me, and I never wanted my time with her to end.

In college, God gave us (Ken and Gabe) a campus minister who would eventually become a great friend and mentor. We all affectionately call him "Big Love," because that's who he is to all of us. There is a list of many others, too significant to name.

Yours might not be called Mama Jane or Big Love, but somewhere along your path, you've been blessed to intersect with someone who seemed like a walking angel to you—like time stood still when that person was there. Being with them was as if they had bottled up a gallon of courage and placed it on the insides of your bone and marrow. You felt like you walked taller, smiled bigger, and had a bit of bounce in your step after being together with them. Their presence filled you with . . . life.

We've often wondered what exactly it is about them that makes us feel this way, and in many cases, it boils down to one thing: they are interested in you—in us. And their interest in us puts fuel in our tanks. Thinking back on times with Mama Jane, Big Love, and so many others who have come alongside us, it would be impossible to number the times they wanted to know about our day, our dreams, our season, our highs and our lows, about our wives and our children. Their interest in us made me want to take great interest in them. It was like a glue that made our relationships strong. Their roles in our lives made one thing completely clear: it is far greater to be interested than interesting.

> *Be careful not to confuse "take interest" with "be interesting."*

It won't surprise you that the next part of our formula is *I*. What in the world does *I* mean here? It's very simple. *I* stands for "take *interest.*" When you go toward people, you take interest in them. Be careful not to confuse "taking interest" with "being interesting." There is a vast ocean of churches and people who are working tirelessly, trying their best to be interesting. We see this all the time, and it's exhausting. We do not need more people and more churches working so hard to be interesting.

Have you ever met someone, and knew right away they were not interested in you? Maybe they nodded their head when you talked, and they put a big smile on their face, but you could tell they really didn't care about what you were saying. They talked about being good with relationships and being in the people business, but over the course of years, they never asked one personal question about family, interest, or work. So, you have to wonder, "Were they really interested?" When you sense that someone is not sincerely interested, it makes you want to be as far away from that person, or their organization, as you can be.

This happens all the time at our churches. Think about this. When you look at a church's website and social media or listen to announcements from stage, what are you hearing and seeing? Is it all about the church? Or is it addressing the needs of the community? If it's always only about the church, you can understand how people can feel as if the church is not interested in them or what they're going through in their lives. This isn't because the church is trying to be uninterested; they're most likely doing this without even realizing it. Here's the good news: once the church realizes they haven't been communicating interest in people, they can take steps to remedy that right away.

Now that we know it's important and have seen practical examples, what are ways you can take interest in people around you? Here are four ways your church can practically take interest:

1. *Ask someone a question.* Think about it this way—when's the last time you just asked somebody a question about themselves or their life?

2. *Listen to them.* Instead of trying to tell them something about you, just learn about them.

3. *Be curious.* It actually stands out to people when you take notice of things that are happening in their lives, in their marriages, with their children, with their hobbies, with their interests.

4. *Repeat back to them later what you learned about them earlier.* Subtly letting new people know that you remember things about them is remarkable.

So, why not learn about them? Imagine how impactful it would be if you not only learned something about them or their life, but the next time you saw them, you brought that topic up again. That's a "wow" moment for a family. They will remember that, "This person came toward me, took interest in me and remembered something about me." That's one thing you can do if you want to effectively build life-giving relationships in your church.

Here is an important note for asking people questions. You need to make sure the church knows there are some questions you would not want to ask. If a question may make someone feel awkward, you want to avoid it. Here are some examples:

- Have you been here before?
- Is this your first time here?
- Have we ever met before?
- Do you have a family?

Questions like these are easy to ask, but they are not very life-giving.

What if everyone in your church asked people certain questions to get to know those who attend for the first time? Questions like:

- Did you grow up in this area?
- What was it like growing up in this area? /What brought you to this area?
- What do you enjoy about what you do for a living?

As you train people about asking good questions, make sure they understand the importance of listening to the answers. This is going to matter as we continue to implement the formula.

$$\frac{G(I + C)}{T} = LGR \times \uparrow P = \text{Culture of LGR}$$

C Stands for "*Connect* People to People"

Leaders of today's church certainly love people—no one would ever deny that. But, loving those people has to look like something tangible in every interaction. Simply smiling and waving at people won't be enough. There must be more. When churches become laser-beam-focused on intentionally introducing people to other like-minded people, the likelihood of those people returning to church will go through the roof.

Next, we have C, which stands for "*connect* people to people." When you go toward people and take interest in them, you are now equipped to link those people with other people who have the same type of interests. As you're listening to someone, all of a sudden, you may hear that they like to play golf, and you'll immediately think about people in your church who are interested in golf. Or, as you're taking interest in listening to people, you may find that a mom really likes to exercise and then think of another mom who likes to exercise. You're able to connect people with people.

Maybe you hear about someone's profession. You hear they're a schoolteacher, lawyer, nurse, or firefighter. Whatever their profession might be, you think about the people in your church who are in that same profession, and you try to get them together in an interest group so that they have a common ground. You're paying attention, so you go toward them. Not only do you go toward them, but you also take an interest in them and listen to their answers to your questions. When you do that, you're better equipped to join people to people.

While it seems like a simple concept, to connect people to people, when you evaluate your church, you may notice that we are quick to try to connect people to programs instead of other people. What many first-time guests hear is, "We offer these programs—you should jump right in!" They feel unnoticed rather than feeling as if people are actually getting to know them.

But when we join people to people, it makes a larger church feel small. Now, you may say, "Well, our church is already small." A first-time guest can feel "on the outside" even in a small church. But, if you take the time to listen to that person and introduce them to someone with a common interest, they can feel like they are beginning to belong to your group, small or not. This can happen really fast.

> *We are quick to try to connect people to programs instead of other people.*

When we join people by their interests and professions, it can make an intimidating setting feel more comfortable and encourage that sense of belonging to develop.

$$\frac{G(I+C)}{T} = LGR \times \uparrow P = \text{Culture of LGR}$$

T Stands for *Time*

Benjamin Franklin, one of America's founding fathers, once said that a penny saved is a penny earned. He also knew that the potential of a penny invested, over time, could eventually be worth much more. "In his will, Franklin left the cities of Boston and Philadelphia 1,000 pounds each (the equivalent of $4,444). He asked that the funds gather interest over the next 200 years and also be used for loans to young craftsmen to help them get established in their trades."[33]

Somewhere in the back of his mind, Franklin understood the power of repetition and time. That's the nature of compound interest. Imagine what happened over the subsequent two centuries. Philadelphia prioritized low-interest loans to individuals, accumulating $2.25 million by 1993, while Boston focused on long-term investment, accumulating almost $5 million. Since the early twentieth century, those hefty yields have funded institutions and programs for those pursuing technical educational and professions.

In explaining compound interest, Franklin quipped, "Money makes money. And the money that money makes, makes money." One of the world's greatest investors, Warren Buffett, once called compound interest one of the three things that made him rich: "(My) wealth has come from a combination of living in America, some lucky genes, and compound interest." And Albert Einstein allegedly referred to compound interest as "the most powerful force in the universe."[34]

This principle of "compounding" doesn't apply only to finance; it operates in relationships, too. Compounding relationships is about people connecting with and caring for other people on an ongoing basis—in other words, going toward people, over time. We take an intentional interest in people over time. We introduce people to like-minded people, over time. As with many things we love most in life, the relationships that proved to be the most impactful across all our lives inevitably required great repetition over time.

> *Relationships happen over time.*

So far, we know to build life-giving relationships, we *go* to where people are. Then we take *interest* in them and *connect* them with other people. This isn't something that just happens once. That brings us to the *T* in our formula. *T* stands for *time*. People in your community don't want to just have another encounter with a person. They want to know that person is going to show up again and again and again.

Like remarkable experiences, life-giving relationships don't happen in a microwave. They happen in a crock pot or on a nice, big smoker. It takes time. Relationships happen over time. When you *go* toward people and take *interest* in them and *connect* them to other people consistently over *time*, you are communicating without words that you're not going to go away.

Your church is saying, "We are going be with you in your high moments to celebrate and embrace each other and be so glad to interact with each other. And we're also going to come toward you, even in your lower moments. We're not going to go away when your life gets hard, when things get difficult, or when circumstances get tough. We're going to show up on good days and bad days. And we're going to do that over time."

As this is happening consistently, people who have visited your church may think, "I hope I run into that person, because they showed up on this occasion. They showed up on that occasion. And I believe that if I go to that church or choose to be a part of that community, they'll show up on that occasion again."

It takes time to build life-giving relationships. You show up again and again, for the highs and the lows. You are consistently there to build life-giving relationships with people.

You find ways to show up outside of Sunday mornings. My (Ken) former youth minister, Harvey, was a wonderful example of this. He had a tremendous impact on my life. Now, many years later, he is still having an impact. What made Harvey so impactful in my life? He was only the youth minister for two years at the church. He was impactful because he showed up—which was all the time. He showed up at the ball field and shot basketball with me and the other youth. He went to eat hamburgers with us. He demonstrated what a vibrant, fun, growing relationship with Jesus Christ looked like by the way he lived his life. He showed up not just on Sundays but all week long. He was consistently there to build life-giving relationships. He gave us his time.

This part of the formula is easy to look over, but it is essential. We may feel so strongly about this because we've gotten to experience it first-hand. Both our families were part of a church that was doing this well. We've seen this happen in many churches who are meeting people and assimilating them into the life of their church. But, this was a personal experience for us. And it wasn't a large church, as you might expect. We were helping with a church-start. The pastor there, Jeff Simmons, really put this principle into play.

We saw the way Jeff led the small congregation that became large and multi-site. We saw the formula, especially this element of *time*, in action. We saw people going toward people, and they were taking interest in people. They were connecting people. They did it over time. And it all equaled the formation of life-giving relationships. We got to be a part of that. We felt like we belonged in this particular church because this formula was in action. It wasn't something that was on a screen, but it was happening in our lives. It was happening because people were willing to do all these things inside of the local church.

Let us give you an even more personal example of the impact this can have. I (Gabe) had moved to town all by myself, and my wife was coming at a later date. I knew absolutely no one in the whole town. Jeff literally met me at the door. While we were talking, Jeff introduced me to someone else and then invited me to lunch. Within a few minutes, I knew two people and had a lunch invite. That moment changed so much for me. Jeff came toward me, took an interest in me, listened to me, and took time with me. He also introduced me to other people who did the same that very day. I went back to that church the next Sunday and knew people. This was huge!

This is also an example of a church leader who is connected and using his connectivity to grow his church. Knowing the people who came to church wasn't a status thing or a checkmark on a list for him. It was about the personal relationships and the people, and that was a huge part of the growth that church experienced.

The impact didn't stop there. Our organization, Connect Ministries, was born out of this small church plant experience. One pastor modeled this formula for us, and the impact is still reverberating in the words you're reading here. Honestly, we could probably stop now, and you could take this formula and build life-giving relationships. But, if we did that, we'd be leaving out one key principle.

$$\frac{G(I+C)}{T} = LGR \times \uparrow P = \text{Culture of LGR}$$

INCREASED PARTICIPATION

Imagine life-giving relationships being so valuable to peoples' lives that they became the standard across your church—a people unwilling to settle for anything less meaningful. If you build life-giving relationships, and you *multiply that times "increased participation,"* you amplify the number of people who are doing this. In other words, it's bigger than just something your outreach pastor can do, or your family pastor can do, or your senior pastor can do, or one class can do, or one department can do. It's more than just one person or one area. It's a mindset of your whole church.

It is not enough for your church staff to practice this formula or for your deacons, elders, or thirty percent of your members to do so. The goal is to have as many people as possible in your church active with this formula. This will take training. You will have to talk about it with your members. They have to know the formula. They have to believe it works and be willing to put it into practice.

$$\frac{Go\,(\,Interest + Connect\,)}{Time} = Life\ Giving\ Relationships$$

$$Life\ Giving\ Relationships \times \uparrow Participation = Culture\ of\ LGR$$

When this formula is put in motion, and all these elements are happening at once, it *creates a culture of building life-giving relationships.*

> *When you increase the number of people participating in this mindset, it's not just one life-giving relationship that develops.*

Recently, while attending the twentieth anniversary celebration of Rolling Hills Community Church, we heard story after story of lives that had been changed because a church body embraced the concept of participating in the mission. It wasn't the story of a few people, or the story of the church staff, or the story of the founding pastor—it was the story of a large group of people who got involved in the lives of people in the community. It was a clear picture of what happens when you have a high percentage of participation.

The goal is to increase the number of people inside your church who are thinking with this principle in mind. When you increase the number of people participating in this mindset, it's not just one life-giving relationship that develops. Instead, it's actually the entire culture of your church.

Imagine your church's reputation in your community being one that causes people to say, "You need to be a part of that church, because when you go to their church, you'll be amazed. People will go toward you. Like, all of them—they'll move toward you. And when they get where you are, they'll take an interest in you and your family. Your family is going to be blown away! When you get to that church, they're going to know your name. They're going to call you by name. They're going to know your interests. And you'll be amazed to find that those people connect with other people who are similar to you—pulling for the same team or having a similar hobby or being in a similar season of life. If you're looking to belong, you can belong at this church, because their church makes it easy for you to belong."

If you follow this formula over time, that can be the reputation and the entire culture of your church. And this is what it looks like—*going* to people, taking an *interest*, and *connecting* them with other people over *time* so that you can form a life-giving relationship. Then, increasing the participation so that the culture of your church is building life-giving relationships with people.

An exercise you can do with your team is sit down and look at all you're doing as a church. Ask yourselves, "How are we going to practically apply these things to what we have scheduled to do in our church? How are we going to practically apply each area of this in each ministry of our church? How are we going to apply this to the programming that

BUILD LIFE-GIVING RELATIONSHIPS

we're doing in our church? How are we going to make this the culture of our church by implementing each area of the formula?" Then, figure out how you're going to train your people. This works best when, through training, you multiply the number of people who can operate with this type of mindset, even when you're not around to do it.

You will find that if you execute this formula, you will effectively meet new people and they'll want to plug into the life of your church, all because you committed to building life-giving relationships.

In Huntsville, Alabama, there is a church that is passionate about meeting new people. In the same city, a single mom waited for a church home she didn't know she needed. In 2021, they met.

Amy and her two boys, Noah and Hudson, were attending a church, but they didn't all feel at home there. They heard about Connect Camps happening at another local church and were so excited to be a part of this week that looked so incredible. Little did they know, they were about to find the church where they all would belong—the church that would feel like home.

Meanwhile, this local church was preparing for camp. They had been pushing that Remarkable Wheel, even through the challenge of feeling overwhelmed. They wanted to reach as many campers and families as possible, but that task seemed so big. They pulled back for a moment to think about the power of reaching one family. Who would be the one family the Lord would bring them? The one family they could come around, embrace, and support. That family was

Amy, Noah, and Hudson. That church went toward that family with the intention of building life-giving relationships, and that's just what happened! Not long after camp, Amy was being baptized in a river by the pastor of the church while Noah was excitedly taking picture after picture of this amazing moment.

This church simply let Amy know she was seen. Being a single mom is hard, and they wanted to be there to support, love, and encourage her. Because this church chose to spend the time and effort to push that Remarkable Wheel, they were able to live out what they felt called to do—reach families in their community. Because of that, Amy's family found their church home.

Take a few minutes and complete the Connect Assessment to gauge your churches effectiveness in Building Life Giving Relationships.

Go to https://www.connect-ministries.com/assessment and enter the code CONNECTEDCHURCH for a free assessment.

CHAPTER FOUR

Ingredient #3— Execute a Clear Plan

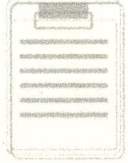

When my (Ken) children were younger, my wife and I decided we needed a heavy-duty wooden swing set with a nice fort area. Since those types of structures are not cheap, we put this big swing set together ourselves instead of paying the professionals to do it. Well, you can probably guess what happened—it took much longer to put together than it should have, and we had boards left over, we had boards cut wrong, we had to buy more wood since we messed up so many boards, we drilled holes in the wrong place, and the list could go on and on. I eventually got it right, but it took much longer and cost more money, because while we tried to follow the plans provided, the plans were not clear to us. It was a frustrating experience, to say the least.

Churches that have an unclear plan or don't have a plan at all create the same type of experience for those who are a part of the church. This is a major barrier to your church meeting new people. This way of operating impacts your church and causes problems for your church in accomplishing its mission.

Problems with Not Having a Clear Plan

Alignment Issues

I (Ken) used to drive a full-size Ford Bronco Eddie Bauer edition a long time ago. It was a man's man type of vehicle, painted black with a tan hard top. You could take off the top and go through the mud. You sat higher than most vehicles on the road—it was the king of the road in my mind. It was good for off-road adventures, and it was good on the interstate. I really loved that vehicle and, to this day, wish I had never sold it.

There was one thing about this Bronco that was not great. When the tires needed to be aligned, this big vehicle shook from top to bottom. The steering wheel and seats would shake, and it would feel like the vehicle was coming apart. You never had to guess what the matter was when this started—you knew—it was time to get the tires aligned. I couldn't handle this shaking vehicle anymore. A vehicle I loved to drive had become difficult and uncomfortable to drive because a major alignment problem with the tires affected the entire experience.

Many churches and organizations have this same type of experience when they do not have a clear plan or do not execute any plan. The church is trying to make progress, but it is shaky, and it feels like the wheels might come off at any time.

> *Alignment ensures church leadership and members go in the same direction.*

Churches must take time to ensure all church leaders are aligned with the church goals before they can expect people to see the church as their support. If people can't see the church as a place of refuge, they won't see past the alignment issues and will miss out on the remarkable experiences.

Without goals and a clear plan, a church rattles and shakes from lack of cohesion. Church programs and ministries become ineffective because the workers don't understand the plan and act at cross purposes. When a church is rattling and the leaders are not aligned, the people focus on the resulting distractions and noise. And when members don't align, there will be distractions as people pull to various ideas. Alignment ensures church leadership and members go in the same direction.

Lack of Unity

When there is no clear plan, it is only a matter of time when the team will lack unity. You will know this is happening because different areas of the church will begin to do their own thing.

The children's ministry will have a strategy, the student ministry will do their own thing, the worship ministry will be working on something completely different, etc. Before you know it, every part of the church is working in silos. This can happen fast, and it happens often in churches when there is no clear plan.

> *Every coach will tell you that for a team to be successful, they must be unified.*

Every coach will tell you that for a team to be successful, they must be unified. Every band director will tell you that for a concert to be successful, all the musicians must play their role and be on the same page of music. In fact, it would be difficult to find any successful organization where the team was not unified around a plan.

Lack of Clarity

Another barrier to meeting new people you will find or may already be experiencing is a lack of clarity. Your church is not meeting new people on a regular basis because the staff and volunteers don't know what the overall plan is for the church. Your plan might be to just reach as many people for Jesus as possible. While that is the ultimate goal, that is too broad. That doesn't provide the needed clarity, and because there is no clarity, progress is stalled. People desire to know where the organization is headed and how they can believe God is leading them to get there.

Breakdown of Communication

Have you ever shown up to volunteer for another organization or event, and when you got there, you were unsure what to do, where to go, what your role was in making this event successful, or who the leader was? Because there was no plan, or at least not a plan that was communicated appropriately, you probably left that event frustrated and defeated. That is what happens in churches when there is no plan.

When leaders do not have a clear plan, it causes tremendous confusion and impacts your church's ability to meet new people. You will struggle to keep members engaged and willing to volunteer and that is a barrier to meeting new people.

People Are Busy, Not Productive

As a leader, have you ever felt like everyone seems too busy to try anything new? You hear things like, "We just don't have any time for that," "I have too much on my plate," or "Someone else will have to do that."

Many times, when there is no clear plan, people get busy doing things that don't matter or at least don't contribute to the organizational goals. Executing a clear plan will define the things that staff and volunteers need to give their time to.

Without a clear plan, a person can waste a lot of time and feel like they are so busy.

THE VALUE OF A CLEAR PLAN

Did you know that fifty thousand people usually run the New York City Marathon every year? That's a lot of people![35] What's even more interesting is that about five hundred of the runners who start the marathon do not finish; they quit for various reasons. However, statistics tell us that about 1.1 million people finish a marathon every year. What is the key to finishing? Why do some people cross the finish line while others come up short?

When many people think of running a marathon, it seems like an overwhelming task. I (Ken) felt the same way until a friend showed me the best way to go about it—executing a clear plan. This plan took sixteen weeks and detailed exactly what I should do each week. I knew exactly how much to run or rest every day. When my friend shared that plan with me, he said, "If you'll follow this plan, you'll be able to finish a marathon in sixteen weeks."

So, I followed the plan and ran the marathon. As I was running, it became obvious that some people didn't follow a plan, or the plan they followed didn't prepare them for the race. It was common to see people getting a golf-cart ride or sitting in the medical tent, not able to finish.

You see, everybody is passionate about finishing at the beginning of the race. Passion alone won't get you to the finish

Execute a Clear Plan

line, but passion and a clear plan can. Passion and plan need to go together. *Passion with no plan leads to poor results.*

When it comes to churches, every church is going to be passionate about meeting new people. Some churches we coach refer to their plan, but it's really a mission or vision statement. It's not a clear plan. *As we study the results from our Connect Assessment, it becomes clearer that the number one area for improvement is executing a clear plan.*

> *Passion with no plan leads to poor results.*

Imagine your church is a boat with everyone rowing. If you are working together, executing a clear plan, those oars are cutting through the water smoothly and in perfect time and rhythm as you are successfully navigating toward your goal.

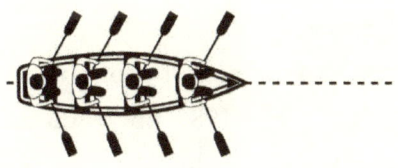

But quite often, the image looks much more like a boat that's heading in the right direction but veers a little off course. The oars are hitting the water at different speeds now. The water is rough, and the boat is getting tossed around pretty good. The next thing you know, people are falling out of the boat, getting hit in the head with oars. The boat is heading in a direction it was never intended to go. The momentum is stalled. Nobody knows where they're going, and you're losing team members. You thought you had a plan, but it sure wasn't this.

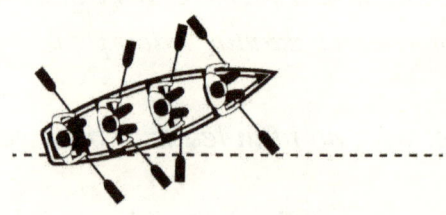

It is not uncommon for organizations to start moving so fast that they fail to notice that the direction in which they are heading is not the direction they started moving in the beginning. They fail to notice that some people in the boat do not have the best interest of the organization in mind. They begin to row in a manner that causes the organization to slowly veer off course.

Enron Energy is an example of a company that started off in a promising direction in 1985, but by the fall of 2000 was crumbling under its own weight. The story of Enron depicts a company that reached unprecedented heights only to collapse with a dizzying speed: "At Enron's peak, its shares were worth $90.75. When it declared bankruptcy on December 2, 2001, shares traded at $0.26." [36] Enron Energy had people rowing the boat, the organization, in the wrong direction. There was not alignment at the top of the organization, and that filtered throughout the organization, leading ultimately to the collapse of the business.

It's likely we all can understand what that's like in the context of our churches. When we're not executing a clear plan, a positive result is either coincidence or luck. To consistently have impactful results, you need a clear plan with everyone on board. So, let's talk practically about how your church can execute a clear plan. This strategy template can serve as blueprint to help your church navigate the team from the burden to achieving the vision God has placed on your heart.

> **Action 1: Name Your Burden**

Executing a clear plan begins with naming your burden. God has wired you and your team to have a heart that's tender in a particular area. This is something God gave you, that He birthed in you. We're not talking about pet peeves or things you might rant about on social media. It's so much more than that. To identify your burden, you may start by asking yourself some questions. What is something inside you that you cannot stand, that is not right? What is something God has placed you and your team on the earth and in your church to address? What wrong do you have a divinely inspired passion to right? What has God impressed on your heart? What is your burden? What is your "why?"

When you have a burden and you share it with the team around you, you'll be closer to answering your "why." How strong is your "why?" How passionate are you about your "why," and how are you doing something about it? Why are you here? If your church is full of people doing lots of things, but none of them can clearly name why they are doing them. Eventually, frustration and weariness will overtake passion and commitment. But, when you have named your burden and shared it with the team around you, you are operating out of a tender heart. That will sustain you in both the good times and the bad times.

Once you have identified your burden and shared it with those around you, the next step is to research your community as it relates to your burden. What do you need to know about your community? What could you study about your community? The more you know about your community and those you're trying to reach, the better you'll be able to put your burden into action in the right direction.

You name your burden and research your community to become informed about the needs that exist around you. You need this information before you form your plan to guard you from false assumptions. Researching about your burden in your particular community does the following:

- Identifies needs
- Identifies trends
- Identifies the demographics

You now have a mindset that has your burden and the needs of the community at the forefront. This mindset helps you make decisions that equip your church to more effectively reach people in your community and plug them into the life of your church.

To help churches do this effectively is our "why" at Connect Ministries. That's why we're here. That's the deep, God-given burden that we have and that we share. That's also why we created the Connect Assessment, which helps churches gauge their effectiveness. This is an amazing tool that equips us to help them meet new people and plug them into the life of their church effectively.

We can see the vital nature of naming your burden and researching it in your community when we look at the lives of extremely effective leaders and organizations. First, let's start with the most important, Jesus Christ. Everything He did was related to His mission—His burden to seek and save the lost.

We don't have the room here to explore His burden in everything He did, but we can consider the woman at the well in Samaria. Jesus didn't have to go through Samaria. As a matter of fact, it was shocking that He made the point not to avoid Samaria. He knew exactly who He would meet at that well. He was so united with the Father's mission that He was always burdened to seek and save the lost. That's what happened with the woman in Samaria, and she shared the Good News with everyone she met!

In the Old Testament, we see Moses with a burden for his people when he sees an Israelite being beaten by an Egyptian. Eventually, that burden becomes part of his calling from God to lead His people out of Egypt. How about Nehemiah? He heard about his people going home and was burdened to rebuild the wall around the city. The king even noticed his burden, and Nehemiah became a huge figure in rebuilding the walls around Jerusalem.

If we look to more recent times in human history, we can learn from Dr. Martin Luther King, Jr., or even an organization like Compassion International. From Dr. King's life, we can see that your burden has to be the anchor of your clear plan, but it also has to be a burden everyone can rally around. His burden was lack of equality and people of color being judged as less-than. That clear burden led to an effective and powerful movement that prompted much change in America and throughout the world.

Compassion International was born from the burden of Reverend Everett Swanson more than seventy years ago. He was in South Korea ministering to American troops fighting in the Korean War. He became burdened by all the war orphans he saw living on the streets in horrible conditions. He saw this burden first-hand and shared it with other Christians when he would preach. He began connecting these Christians who wanted to help with the children who desperately needed their help. Compassion International is now active in twenty-seven countries, helping more than 2.3 million babies, children, and young adults. It all started with a follower of Christ who named his burden.[37]

Everyone in your organization should be able to name the burden. It will be the fuel for the team when the waters get choppy and difficult. You can always go back to the burden and remember why you are doing this in the first place.

> *It is not enough to have a burden as a church leader—you have to ask God to give you the vision for the ministry you are leading.*

Action 1: Name Your Burden

Action 2: Identify Your Vision

As leaders, it is important for us to open our eyes so that we can see where God is leading us. Remember, it starts with a burden, and out of that burden, God provides the vision—but we have to open our eyes to see. Church leaders can get so busy with the business of ministry that they have no idea what the direction or vision is for their church.

Henry Blackaby in his book *Spiritual Leadership*, said,

> Many pastors are busy working for God without seeking God's direction... Too many Christian leaders assume that because they are leaders, they must set the direction, when in reality God is the only one who knows where His people need to be led.[38]

It is not enough to have a burden as a church leader; you have to ask God to give you the vision for the ministry you are leading.

God burdened Moses with a call to lead His people back to their homeland, their promised land. His burden was real, but he didn't have a chance to see this land until the end of his life: "Then Moses climbed Mount Nebo from the plains of Moab to the top of Pisgah, across from Jericho. There the Lord showed him the whole land—from Gilead to Dan, all of Naphtali, the territory of Ephraim and Manasseh, all the land of Judah as far as the Mediterranean Sea, the Negev and the whole region from the Valley of Jericho, the City of Palms, as far as Zoar. Then the Lord said to him, "This is the land I promised on oath to Abraham, Isaac and Jacob when I said, 'I will give it to your descendants.' I have let you see it with your eyes, but you will not cross over into it." (Deuteronomy 34:1–4 NIV).

> *Vision that is birthed out of a burden is the foundation to executing a clear plan.*

Execute a Clear Plan

Sometimes, as leaders, we have to take those we lead to the mountaintop and "open the window," asking them what they see. Look out over the horizon and ask God, "What do you want me to see out there? What do you want me to do about it? Where are we going?" Those are the actions of a leader who has vision. Where do you see our organization heading in six months? Twelve months? Three years? Five years? Ten years?

> *A vision without a burden might take your church in a direction you—and, more importantly, God—never intended for it to go.*

It will be different for every organization based on the leader and the timing in the organization. Sometimes, organizations need a very clear twelve-month vision that helps them navigate through tough waters. Other times, you come out of a twelve-month vision, and now your church is ready to "see out the window" much further. There is no formula that says every church needs to have a certain timeframe on their vision, but every church should have a vision of some length in written form. Vision that is birthed out of a burden is the foundation to executing a clear plan.

As important as vision is, it is for good reason that you don't start with vision. If vision were the starting place, you'd be tempted to lead a team of people, all giving their opinions on a variety of directions you could choose to go. A vision without a burden might take your church in a direction you—and, more importantly, God—never intended for it to go. But, done in the right order, your team can operate out of a deep burden for your community. You can share a picture of a beautiful future that gives you, as leaders, the opportunity to say, "I imagine today that we could head in this direction." If you want to execute a clear plan, it starts with naming your burden and identifying the vision that God's laying on your heart.

THE BENEFITS OF VISION— AND HOW TO CAST A VISION

If you have ever been in the room when a leader casts a vision, you know firsthand the benefits of a vision for an organization. First, a vision can provide *alignment*. Vision tells everyone in the organization that this is the direction we are heading. Without a vision, the team can wander around and not know where they are heading and how they will get there. Second, a vision can *energize* a team. When people hear where the organization is heading, they can rally around that vision and give them tremendous energy, which can create momentum. Third, vision gives an organization the *willingness to take calculated risks*. If the vision can be accomplished without taking risks and trusting God for His intervention, then the vision is too small. Lastly, vision gives forward motion. It paints the picture that, while we have seen God do a lot in our church, we are moving forward. We have more to accomplish for the kingdom. We will learn from the past, but we are not going to live in the past—we are moving forward.

Casting Vision

As leaders identify their vision and understand the benefits, their next step must be to cast and articulate that vision. A vision that no one knows about robs the organization of the many benefits of a vision. Here are some quick tips for articulating your vision:

1. Articulate it clearly.
2. Articulate it constantly.
3. Articulate it creatively in every avenue of communication that you have.

Timing and methodology will be important in casting your vision to people. Leaders should think in terms of concentric circles when they make the vision public. Start with the smallest circle of people or insiders—these could be the pastors or pastoral team. Then, gradually work outward, making sure you have buy-in to the vision in every circle before moving to the next circle.

Once you have engaged your inner circle of a few key leaders, your church can move to a larger circle of individuals from various ministries. As more people get on board with your church's vision and goals, the circle expands until eventually, you reach the people who are attending church but not actively serving in one of your ministry areas. The idea is that they will go out into the community to bring more people in because they caught the vision. Perhaps your church could have a short, simple slogan that is repeated every week during the sermons and used in social media hashtags.

DON'T CONFUSE MISSION, VISION, AND STRATEGY

But if you stopped at identifying and articulating your vision, you'd be left with a big gap between where you are and where you want to go. Often, the churches we talk to are pretty good at naming their burden and even talking about their vision, but the next step isn't as certain.

Many times, we identify this uncertainty by asking, "Hey, what's your strategy?" We may hear things like, "Well . . . it's to love and love people." That statement is really about their mission; it is not a clear plan. It's awesome that they have a burden for lost people, which is very healthy. A mission to love God and love people is beautiful as well.

In short, many churches stop after mission–vision. They put their mission on the wall and share their vision with the church body but never take the time to assemble a detailed plan that describes how the church will get there. Churches will share with us their mission or vision when we ask about their strategy, but there is great confusion around strategy and strategic plans.

EXECUTE A CLEAR PLAN

The question that will take churches from the burden to achieving the vision is, "How?" How do we move from the burden to accomplishing the vision?

> **Action 1: Name Your Burden**
>
> **Action 2: Identify Your Vision**
>
> **Action 3: Determine and Create Your Strategy**

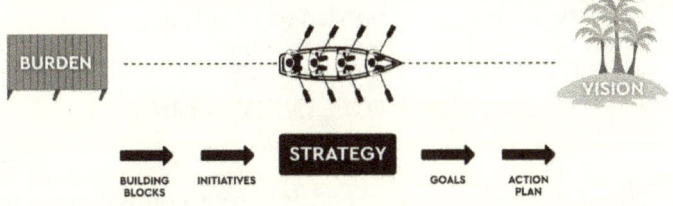

Naming your burden answers the question, "Why?" Identifying your vision answers the question, "Where?" When it comes to strategy, the questions are "What?" and "How?"

We move from burden to vision with a strategy. It sounds simple, but most organizations struggle with strategy because this is where the bulk of the work happens. Strategy involves extremely detailed work that takes a lot of time to implement. As a church leader, you've probably already experienced this challenge. You're so busy with so many things, it's hard to also do the strategic work and get all the volunteers adequately trained so that everyone is on the same page as it relates to your church's strategy.

> *We move from burden to vision with a strategy.*

We know determining and implementing your strategy is a tall order. So, we want to share a simple template for strategy that has worked for us and for other organizations as well. We are convinced that if you took this strategy template and put it in place, it would be easy for you to execute and implement it in your church. Your strategy would play its part and help you move from your burden to your vision.

AN EASY-TO-USE STRATEGIC PLANNING TEMPLATE

The strategy we recommend is a four-component template. The first component is to *identify your building blocks*.

Step 1—Identify Your Building Blocks

Now, you may say, "Okay, what are building blocks?" Building blocks are the fundamental areas at the core of your ministry. Maybe your building blocks are things that are key to your children's ministry or your overall church ministry. For instance, specific time slots could be considered building blocks, such as Sunday morning or Saturday night worship.

Another building block may be your small group Bible studies, new construction, a new ministry area you want to grow, or an international ministry. These are examples of areas that would help you say, "We're putting our emphasis on these things for the upcoming period of time. We're focusing on these areas now."

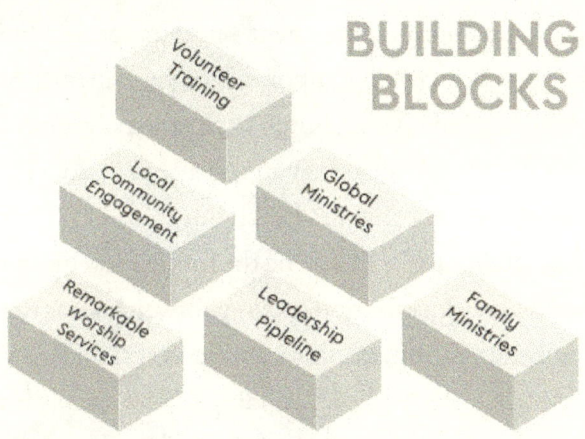

There is no correct number of building blocks. Leaders will want to be careful not to have too many, because it is impossible to emphasize over six. We would recommend about four to six building blocks, with churches giving tremendous focus to those areas. Also, every church will not have the same building blocks. You will build your entire strategy around these blocks, which will help your church achieve its vision in a determined number of years.

It's important that you identify your specific building blocks and that your church leadership team agrees with you. The building blocks your church identifies will inform how you write out your initiatives. If there is no agreement on the building blocks, then it's going to be extremely difficult to move forward.

To get unanimous agreement on your specific building blocks, you may have to temporarily or permanently remove some familiar things your church has historically done. When you do this, you can all agree you will all have a concentrated focus on these areas of your church now.

These building blocks will be the foundation upon which you build your organization moving forward. Your time, energy, communication, calendar, and resources will go toward these building blocks. Your building blocks establish where your focus will be for a period of time. If an idea is proposed that is outside the scope of your current building blocks, the answer might not be "No," but instead, "Not right now."

Execute a Clear Plan

Step 2: Identify Your Initiatives

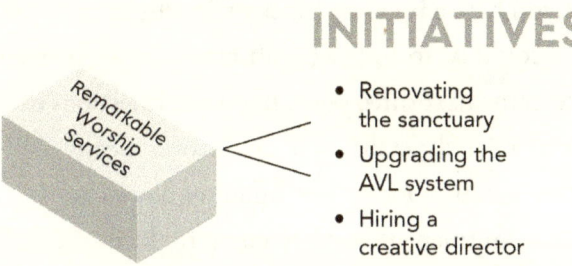

After you have identified your building blocks, it's time to quickly move to the second component: *identify your initiatives.* Again, your question might be, "Okay, what's an initiative?" An initiative is anything that is going to take approximately two or three years to implement. It's not a quick fix; it takes a bit of time to get it worked into the pattern of the church. In many cases, although not all, it requires additional resources. To determine your initiatives, you can ask things like, "What are those things that will require additional resources and take a couple of years to work into the flow of our church?"

For example, if one of your building blocks is "missions," an initiative could be an international mission trip. For a "children's ministry" building block, an initiative could be to remodel your children's ministry facilities in the next five years. If you have a building block of "next-gen ministry," an initiative could be to add two staff members to the next-gen ministry in the next three years. If anyone questions these initiatives or related details, you can answer clearly, "We are doing this because one of our building blocks is ____. We made a commitment that we're going to do this to support our building block." Everyone knows what you're doing and why you're doing it.

When you identify your building blocks and initiatives, then you can decide, as a church, what you will focus on, how you will budget, and how you will plan. It will be clear that if you do these things, it will help you accomplish your building blocks and initiatives and will also allow you to write your goals—and it is beyond important that you have goals.

Step 3: Identify Your Goals

That is the third component of this strategy: *identify your goals.* There are many opinions about how to write effective goals. It is not enough to simply have goals, because they need to be written similarly across the organization.

Connect Ministries has found the model of S.M.A.R.T. goals to be the most effective goal-setting format.

S.M.A.R.T. goals were developed by George Doran, Arthur Miller, and James Cunningham in their 1981 article, "There's a S.M.A.R.T. way to write management goals and objectives." Specific, Measurable, Attainable, Realistic, and Timely (S.M.A.R.T.)[39]

Specific. What are you trying to do? Who is going to be part of the team? Why are you trying to do this? Where is what you are trying to do taking place? When will you do what you need to do? Be specific, provide a clear picture, and hold people accountable.

Measurable. How will you measure what you are doing? Is it by the number of people attending an event, the number of people navigating your webpage? How will you assess your achievement?

Attainable. With the tools that you have, can you reach your goal? If not, what do you need? If you are trying to fundraise to buy winter coats for two hundred children, can you obtain the amount of money needed to purchase the coats? Can you find donors or establish a partnership with a local store?

Realistic. Can you actually meet the goals you are setting forth? Using the same example, if you only have three people in your organization, how much time and effort can the three of you give to fundraise for two hundred coats? If the objective is not realistic, what do you need to do to make it so, or do you need to change the objective?

Timely. What is the timeline to meet your goals? Work backward. Start with your final objective and plan backward to create an outline. Backward planning gives the big picture and helps identify all that needs to get done. Logistics can be tricky: transportation, room reservations, requisitions, purchases, and advertising all require work in advance.

As a church, identify three to five goals you're working toward together.

Types of Goals Needed for Different Ministries in the Church

Church-wide	3-5 annual goals
Individual Ministries	Need 3-5 goals specific to your ministry (student, worship, children's, etc.)
Individual Staff/Volunteers	Need 3-5 goals that support the initiative and building blocks

Everyone in your church ought to know what the overall goals are for the church. Even more than that, each department should identify specific goals as well: children's

EXECUTE A CLEAR PLAN

ministry, student ministry, college ministry, women's ministry, men's ministry. When every department has individual goals that are aligned with your church's overall goals, they will help your church fulfill your initiatives and support your building blocks. This is when you will see the strategy working.

In addition to the larger organizational and department goals of your church, it's also wise to consider individual goals. Does everyone on your church staff have yearly goals they can articulate? Do they build upon one another? Do they support the initiatives your church is trying to implement? Do they contribute to fulfilling the foundational parts of your ministry, your building blocks? When you sit down with a staff member or a team member, can they articulate, "I'm doing these things to support the ongoing further development of our strategy"?

> *Remember that goals are for motivation and alignment. They are never meant to be used as a hammer or for punishment.*

The formation of individual supporting goals isn't only applicable to your full-time staff. Have you ever thought about asking your volunteers what goal or goals they might have for the ministry in which they serve? Goals, whether they be organizational, departmental, or individual, can be a crucial part of making your identified initiatives happen.

It's easy to get off track with goals. Remember that they are for motivation and alignment, a tool to help you have a plan that aligns with your vision. Goals are never meant to be used as a hammer or for punishment.

On occasion, you may find that circumstances change and you need to reassess or modify your original goal. You may also conclude you had too many things to work toward. When reaching the goal feels more like a chore than something to be excited about, then it is time to reevaluate.

> We discuss this in detail through our Connect Assessment and Coaching. We will help you identify practical and achievable goals, but keep the purpose of the goals always in the forefront of our minds.

Step 4: Create Your Action Plans

Once you have identified your goals, it's time for the next step. The fourth component of our strategy is: *create your action plans.* Have you ever sat down and created a timeline for everything that your department or your part of the organization needs to do to make sure that the goals happen? Have you made an action plan to ensure your initiatives happen and to ensure the building blocks are getting the support they need?

It takes a lot of work to construct these action plans, but it is more than worth it. When you invest the time and effort, it gives everybody in the organization, whether volunteer or full-time staff, accountability, making sure that you're all moving in the same direction. For example, if you have established the goal to increase volunteers by ten percent in your next-gen ministry, you now need to write down everything that has to happen for you to accomplish that goal. Don't be afraid of details. Be as granular as your mind will allow you to go. Leave no step out. Each action item you list should have a due date and a person responsible for it.

Your action planning, if done correctly, will probably take you several days. Creating a plan this detailed is hard work, and that is why many organizations omit this step, but without this step it will be easy for many important items to be left undone. When this happens, executing a clear plan becomes very difficult.

> **Action 1: Name Your Burden**
>
> **Action 2: Identify Your Vision**
>
> **Action 3: Determine and Create Your Strategy**
>
> **Action 4: Keep Your Team Aligned**

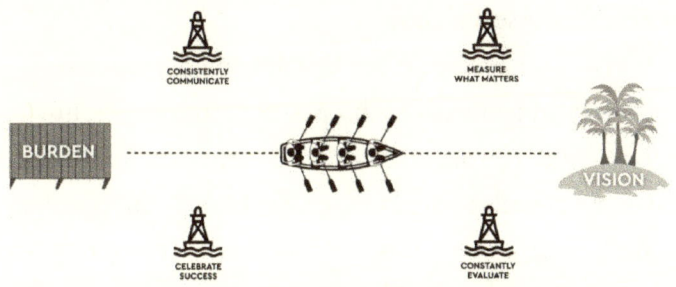

Once you have your strategy in hand, you need navigational buoys to keep your boat in alignment. You don't want to get off course as you seek to achieve your goals.

We've discovered that meeting new people and plugging them into the life of your church won't happen by accident. It's not a coincidence when this takes place. It's the result of a team like yours getting together and executing a clear plan. That starts with naming and sharing your burden with your team and others around you, then having a God-given vision that's a compelling picture of the future. Finally, you answer the strategy question, "How are we going to move from our burden to achieving our vision?" That's what a clear plan looks like.

Once you've got your plan, it's always smooth sailing from there, right? No. Not always. It may happen that when you've got all these things in place and begin executing your clear plan, at some point, your boat could begin to slowly veer off course. Before you realize it, you're moving away from your vision. You think to yourself, "We just landed on this plan, and I thought we were all on the same page. How did we get off course like this?"

When this happens, it can feel discouraging and frustrating. If you find yourself in this position, trust us on this: you are not alone. You are not weird. You are not a failure. Every leader of a church or organization has been in this position.

We'll share about a time we found ourselves in this position. In 2010, Connect Ministries launched Connect Race, an event to help churches meet new people in their community.

Over the next seven years, we conducted over 150 races with over 100,000 runners. We were doing 5Ks, 10Ks, and half-marathons. When you hear those numbers, it might lead you to say that resource was highly effective.

But we ended up cutting it in 2018. The reason? We had drifted off mission. We partnered with businesses in communities where we had races, and those businesses were getting more exposure than the churches we were also partnering with. We realized the churches were not getting the opportunity to really meet anyone. Helping the churches meet new people was our whole purpose, and it wasn't happening. While we had a lot of runners, we had a mission drift. We got out past our navigational buoys and had to get our boat back on course.

So, what do you do when your plan is in place but your boat gets a little off course? We suggest you put four buoys in place to ensure you all keep moving forward, executing your clear plan. When you bump up against these buoys, it will put your plan right back in motion, the way you intended for it to be:

Buoy Number One: Communicate Consistently. This is one thing you can do to help your church or organization stay on course. Communicate consistently. Consistently communicate. And then communicate again. And then communicate again. And then keep communicating, again and again and again.

Communicate about what? Well, go back to your plan. Share your burden again. And then share your burden again.

And lead from a tender heart. A team stays on the same page because they communicate about their burden. They cast the vision again. And then cast the vision again. And then communicate it by video, and then by email, and then from stage, and then through texts. Communicate again and again and again.

Communicate about your strategy. Post your strategy visually. Announce your strategy verbally. Go over the strategy. Make sure everybody can articulate the goals. Go over the goals again. Talk through your timeline again. Communicate consistently. When this first guardrail is in place, all areas inside your church are equipped to know what the clear plan is and help you execute it.

Buoy Number Two: Measure What Matters. We have found this to be vitally important in our own organization. We have scoreboards in different places in our office. They're not scoreboards like you would see on a baseball or football field. They are scoreboards that track things that really matter to our organization: things that support our strategy so that the vision can take place. When you put a scoreboard in place for volunteers and staff to see, it reminds them what is really important to you as a leadership team and to your church. You are more likely to stay on course while executing your plan when you consistently measure what matters.

For example, one area that's easy to measure is the effectiveness of your digital presence. When was the last time you measured your followship? Your engagement? Your click-through rate? Your views? Your comments? If increasing your digital presence is a goal, you'll want to have weekly measurements to help your church meet that goal.

Buoy Number Three: Celebrate Success. It seems so simple, but often leaders get so busy they forget to celebrate. When you have this buoy in place, you stop from time to time and tell your team, "We just experienced a win! We used to be here and now we're here. We're making progress. We've got a way to go, but we have made progress from where we used to be."

If all you do is go, go, go, and never stop to celebrate, eventually, your people will tucker out. It's tiring to execute a clear plan and never stop to celebrate the progress that you're making. When you stop and celebrate, it's refreshing for you and your team. Every time you stop and celebrate, you're reminding your team that it's worth it to keep going and to stay on course. When you celebrate success, your team will be even more invigorated and energized to execute the plan you've put in place.

Celebrating success also means reminding your team what's important. If you talk about a goal every week and then, months later, you reach that goal, but you don't take time to celebrate the success of reaching that goal, your team will wonder if it was really important to begin with. If it's important enough to be a goal, then it should be important enough to celebrate milestones in pursuit of the goal or when you complete the goal itself.

Buoy Number Four: Constantly Evaluate. Have you noticed that organizations all around you are constantly asking for feedback? Drive-throughs, groceries, fitness clubs—they're always on the search for feedback. Apps on your smart phone ask you to rate them (if not now, then later). All these organizations are looking for feedback and evaluation.

So, why is it that the church, which is the most important organization in the world, chooses not to regularly get feedback from its leaders and members? Constantly evaluating can help your church stay on course.

And by constantly, we mean constantly. This is an all-year-long process. Effective evaluation is more than evaluating after an event. While that is important, you actually need to evaluate all year long. By doing this, it will help keep your church from drifting away from the strategy you've worked so hard to build.

One way you can constantly evaluate is by creating an evaluation document where staff and volunteers can go input their ideas any time of year. For instance, they may leave a Sunday morning service thinking, "Man, what if we did such and such?" It is a win for you to have a system in place for them to share that evaluation with you, as the leader, in real time.

Another element of evaluation is surveying. For your children's ministry, you can survey the parents and even the children. For student ministry, you can survey the students. You can survey whatever age group you're working with. This will help you keep your thumb on the pulse of what people are saying and doing and thinking inside your church or organization, and it creates a mindset of constant evaluation.

Regarding evaluation or survey forms, it's important to remember that surveys don't need to take ten minutes to complete. Most of the time, you can get the information you need from three to five questions, with one place to offer written feedback. For church ministries, we recommend a short survey once a quarter for your ministry that goes to parents or participants.

When you put these buoys in place, it will keep you on your strategy and help your organization stay on course.

Take Your Turn

When you see a team successfully executing a clear plan, you notice that everybody is working in the same direction, and they are gaining a lot of ground. It almost looks effortless. But, we've learned together that it takes a team a lot of work to get to the place of executing a clear plan.

It's a lot of information that we've gone through. Really, the work should occur within three main categories.

First, you name your God-given burden and identify your vision.

Second, move forward with a well-defined strategy. It doesn't matter what strategy template you use. We've seen our strategy template be effective, but you may have identified a strategy that will work better for you. The point is that you have a well-defined strategy that people across the church understand.

Finally, make sure you have some intentional buoys in place to help your church stay on course to see the vision God gave you become a reality.

You've learned all about executing a clear plan, and now it's your turn. It's your turn to build your own template. Here's what we encourage you to do: as a team, as a group of volunteers, as your staff gets together, write down your burden and your vision. This could be the burden and vision for a particular area or ministry within your church or for the church at large. Write down your burden and your vision. Spend time asking what your burden is and identifying the vision that God wants you to head toward for the future. Then, build a template and fill in the blanks with each of the components of this plan. When you do that, you'll be on your way to executing a clear plan.

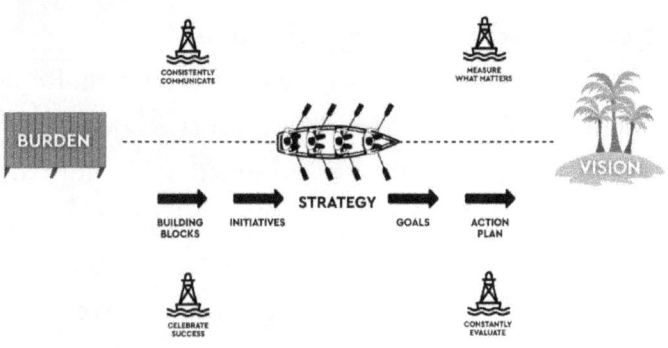

Executing a Clear Plan Produces Results

Connect Ministries had just started. We had a burden, and we had a vision with many ideas. We were doing three-on-three basketball tournaments to help churches meet new people, and we had the dream of launching day camps that would help the church meet new people in their community.

In God's sovereignty, we had the blessing of meeting with John and Trudy White. That began a friendship that God has used to continue to shape this ministry. No other relationship has been more impactful on the formation of Connect Ministries. Very early in our friendship, we learned the importance of executing a clear plan and how to create a strategy that actually helped our organization accomplish the God-given vision. Much of this chapter is taken from the time we spent with them, learning and executing a clear plan.

How do we know that executing a clear plan produces results? We know because we have seen that happen here at Connect Ministries. Since 2006, we have helped over 2000 churches, we have had 300,000 campers attend Connect Camps, we have had 150,000 participants attend one of our Connect Events, 15,000 salvations, and over 30,000 unchurched people ask for a local church to follow up with them about the person of Jesus Christ.

It is true that executing a clear plan alone is not enough—it is the work of God through His plan that produces results. But, it is the responsibility of the leader to execute the plan to address the church's burden.

Every leader is interested in results. We want to celebrate the results that indicate we are fulfilling our vision, and we want to learn from the results that indicate the areas for improvement. Once you state that burden, God will produce a vision that He wants you and your church to attack. Once you have those nailed down, your strategic plan should be placed right in the middle of the two. When this is done, you will be well on your way to executing a clear plan.

Take a few minutes and complete the Connect Assessment to gauge your churches effectiveness in Executing a Clear Plan.

Go to https://www.connect-ministries.com/assessment and enter the code CONNECTEDCHURCH for a free assessment.

CHAPTER FIVE

Ingredient #4—
Enjoy Deep Friendship with God

Ribeye. Steak. What was your first reaction to reading those words? If you're like me, you immediately pictured a big, juicy, marinated, caramelized, marbled, beautiful steak. Maybe you started to get hungry.

It is a special anticipation when you know friends are coming over, and you are finally going to cut into that steak you have marinated and lovingly prepared. You absolutely cannot wait to eat it. You're so excited! And when you do cut into it, oh my goodness. You think to yourself, "I didn't even need a knife for this!" It is nice and juicy; there's even butter running over the side of it. Everyone at the table is talking about how good this steak is. All the preparation that went into getting that ribeye to just the right level of tenderness and juiciness was worth it, a total labor of love.

But that's not always the case. I (Gabe) once heard about a steakhouse that would serve me the best steak I had ever eaten. That is quite a claim. Of course, I think the best steaks I've ever eaten have come right off my own grill. But I kept hearing, "You have to go! You've just *got* to go there!" So, maybe it would be the best steakhouse steak ever. I just had to try it.

I went to the steakhouse—the very expensive steakhouse. The service was excellent. The appetizer was great. The bread was good. The salad was . . . salad. It was fine, too. But, I was ready for the main event. Ribeye. Steak.

The anticipation my family and I felt for all the tender and juicy goodness that was coming was quickly dissipated by the first cuts into the meat. The steaks were dry—dry as a bone. Where was the tender and juicy goodness? Where was the cascade of butter off the side? Nowhere. Those things were nowhere. It was the steak version of the desert. I felt like my jaw was going to break, eating that tough, dry ribeye. My muscles started cramping up. I thought about breaking out the ibuprofen but instead asked for the menu to be sure I hadn't accidentally ordered beef jerky.

There is nothing worse than looking forward to a steak only to realize it wasn't marinated, wasn't cooked right, and is dry as a bone—to expect steak but instead get jerky.

No steakhouse has ever become famous for serving dry steaks. What does this have to do with all the things we've been talking about?

Spiritual Dryness

You're a church that's trying to meet new people right now. You want to plug those people into the life of your church. Obviously, you would never want to serve people a dry church, a dry experience full of people who are dry in their hearts.

But often, the more you get into ministry and leadership in the church, the more and more you get pulled in a lot of different directions. You find out you spend more time than you ever anticipated being spiritually dry. We know that's difficult. It's difficult to create, to build, the type of church that can effectively meet new people when the people in the church are spiritually dry.

Likewise, it's hard to meet new people when the church is being led by spiritually dry leaders. There is little doubt that when the leader is spiritually dry, it impacts the entire church. We see the ripple effects of spiritually dry leaders everywhere. Sometimes, it looks like moral failure. We can also see it manifest as laziness or apathy. It may look like a lack of vision or many other unhelpful traits.

If you're like most leaders in Scripture and in the history of the church, then you know this tension all too well. No one has to describe burnout to you—you've tasted it. No one has to tell you the dangers of isolation—you've either witnessed it or lived it yourself. No one has to describe what it feels like to have little to no spiritual substance to offer or what it's like for your heart to grow bitter, callous, or numb—you might even be there right this very minute.

You know exactly what it's like to have a heart be drained of intimacy and eyes robbed of wonder about what God is doing all around you. Because you've walked this path before, you know just what Henry Blackaby meant when he said, "Spiritual blindness leads to missing God's activity, no matter how evident it is."[40] You and I both know it's nearly impossible to join God in the work He's doing when you're admittedly dry as a bone.

> *God desires to be in deep friendship with man, and He longs for man to be in deep friendship with Him.*

As we have worked with churches all over the country for many years, we have found that one of the most important ingredients of a church that effectively meets new people is having leaders and church members who enjoy deep friendship with God. This is the antidote to spiritual dryness.

PREACHING TO THE CHOIR

As a church leader, no one has to tell you how important a life of spiritual vitality is. That is, after all, the main thing you are seeking to do: introduce people to life in Jesus and then help them grow in that new spiritual life with Him.

You are probably thinking, "Well, of course. I know the importance of a deep friendship with God. I've been called to ministry. I'm seminary-trained, and this is what I do for a living. I teach people how to do this. You're kind of preaching to the choir here." You may already be thinking about Jeremiah 29:12–13 (one of the passages believers refer to over and over): "Then you will call on me and come and pray to me, and I will listen to you. You will seek me and find me when you seek me with all your heart" (NIV). God makes this promise to His people, "I will be found by you." He's insinuating from the very beginning that He desires to be in deep friendship with man, and He longs for man to be in deep friendship with Him.

Then, of course, we come to the New Testament. James 4:8 says, "Come near to God and he will draw near to you." Even those who came after Christ were reminding people, "Hey, draw near to God. God desires to walk with you so that you can enjoy that closeness all the days of your life on the earth." We also see Jesus Himself say to His disciples, and eventually to us, "Remain in me, as I also remain in you" (John 15:4 NIV).

Jesus desires for us to be in deep friendship with Him so that we can know what intimacy with God looks like on a daily basis. You know this, but you also know you're being pulled in a thousand different directions. Even when you know Scripture, it's like a huge game of tug-of-war, and your heart is being tugged all over the place. Because of that, it is possible for you to work for God but not actually walk with Him on a daily basis.

You may even know all the stats that warn of this reality. Here are some of them:

- Over seventy percent of ministers work between fifty-five and seventy-five hours a week.[41] Can you relate to that? Are you thinking, "I work all the time. In fact, I feel like I'll never get a day off?"[42]

- Over twenty-five percent of ministers do not communicate regularly with a trusted colleague or friend.[43] And seventy percent of pastors say they don't *have* a trusted friend.[44] Think about that—trying to have deep friendship with God but lacking any close friendship with another human being.

- Eighty percent of pastors feel like pastoral ministry affected their families negatively.[45]

- Seventy percent of ministers say they have a lower self-esteem now, compared to when they started in ministry.[46]

- Somewhere between 250 and 1,500 pastors (yes, 1,500) leave their churches each month due to moral failure, spiritual burnout, or contention in their church.[47]

> *It is possible for you to work for God but not actually walk with Him on a daily basis.*

The paradoxical truth is that ministry can leave you spiritually dry. And that results in spiritually dry church leaders.

And spiritually dry church leaders often, if not always, have a spiritually dry church.

PLANNING TO OVERCOME SPIRITUAL DRYNESS

So, we're left with the question, "How in the world do we address this?" If we want to become the type of church that meets new people, what do we do about this tension that we're facing? Well, one thing we know is that the unchurched people you are trying to meet aren't interested in being a part of a spiritually dry church. When they're on the outside looking in and notice a group of people walking around like zombies, they can tell there is very little life inside the church. That's not going to cause unchurched people to say, "Yeah, let's be a part of that," or, "Man, I wish that's what my life was like."

We need to deal with this question: "How do you lead a church to walk in deep friendship with God so that others on the outside will be inspired to do the same?" We know you want to do that so you can effectively meet those people and eventually plug them into the life of your church.

We're going to share three questions that will be instrumental in helping you, personally, to walk in deep friendship with God and help others in your church do the same.

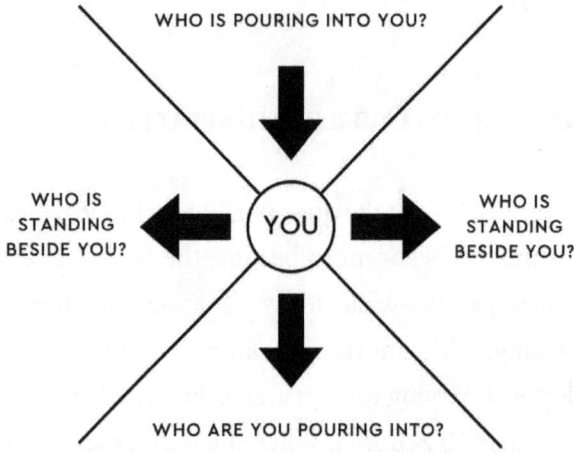

We're going to put you right in the middle of these three questions. So, put your name right there in the middle of that *X*. You, as a leader who is enjoying deep friendship with God, are right in the middle. Now, let's fill in these three questions that should surround you. They are three questions you can ask so you can put yourself right in the middle of this *X*.

Enjoy Deep Friendship with God

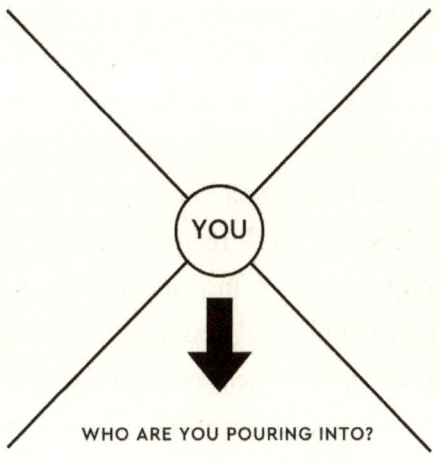

Who Are You Pouring Into?

Question 1: Who are you pouring into? It's hard for you to enjoy a deep friendship with God without actively pouring into the people around you. This is, in fact, the very reason you are on the earth. In the Great Commission, Jesus is literally telling us, "You go, and you make disciples." That's His heartbeat for us.

> *We know the things we learn from God are learned on a deeper level when we have the opportunity to pour those things into other people.*

We can look at His life and see how that was His heartbeat when He was here on earth. First, Jesus took time to spend with the Father, and the Father poured into Him. Then, Jesus poured into others. He took His disciples aside, away from the crowds, to teach them. He also taught them by taking them with Him. He sent them out on their own and brought them back. He would teach them and encourage them, not only as a group, but also as individuals. He knew their individual strengths and weaknesses and poured His love, wisdom, guidance, and encouragement into them accordingly. The Father poured into Jesus. Jesus poured into the disciples. And the disciples, in turn, poured into others.

We know the things we learn from God are learned on a deeper level when we have the opportunity to pour those things into other people.

We've all heard it said after a time of ministry, "I thought I was going there for them, but looking back, I'm convinced that no one was impacted more than *me!*" The best learning lessons we've ever had in life were the ones where we were asked to teach to others. Most often in ministry, any time you have to pour something into someone else, you first have to eat it yourself. The greatest learning takes place when you are the one who is forced to teach it first. That is one of the greatest joys of being entrusted with the gift of influence.

In Matthew 25:14–30, we see Jesus tell the Parable of the Talents. In the story, each servant is entrusted with an opportunity, some servants making better on theirs than others. In the end, we are reminded by Jesus that the very happiest way to live is to maximize the opportunities that have been entrusted into our care. Intentionally pouring into others' lives has the potential of being life-changing not only for them but for you, too! Steward your opportunity to influence well.

We would all agree that pouring into others pays huge dividends. We see this lived out every single day in the business world. In his Harvard Business Review article titled, "The Case for Investing More in People," Eric Garton wrote about the importance of keeping the workforce inspired: "An inspired employee is more than twice as productive as a satisfied employee, and more than three times as productive as a dissatisfied employee. Yet, only one in eight employees are inspired."[48]

If that's what happens when workplace leaders invest in their employees, how much more hangs in the balance when church leaders invest in their people? Imagine your time with people serving as a springboard for them to launch into their destiny. You've been entrusted with words, so steward them to cast vision. You've been entrusted with knowledge, so steward it to equip servants. You've been entrusted with influence, so steward your actions as a trusted model. You've been entrusted with listening ears, so steward them with an inspiring voice. You've been entrusted with classrooms, so steward them to teach. You've been entrusted with resources, so steward them to bring heaven to earth through your intentional influence.

Recognize those who are winning. Help those who are hurting. Mentor those who are eager to learn. Intentionally invest in those whom God has entrusted into your care. After all, I'm betting that is one major reason you wanted to get here in the first place.

So, who are you pouring into? Your first thought may be, "I'm pouring into a whole church." We encourage you to be more specific than that. Think about specific individuals in your church you are actually pouring into. Name those people. Rather than just saying, "I'm pouring into a children's ministry or a youth ministry or into a congregation," name specific people you are specifically and intentionally pouring into. What are the things that you're going to teach them? What are some things God's doing in your life that you can promote in the lives of other people, so they may be able to say, "I'm here. I'm beginning to hear what God is saying, and I know what God wants me to do about it. I'm learning what God is saying because you're teaching me, and I'm learning from you what God wants me to do about it."

When you pour into people in that way, over time, they experience spiritual growth in their own lives, all because you became intentional about asking the first question, "Who are you pouring into?" When you name the people you want to pour into, then you're multiplying people who will be enjoying deep friendship with God. Think about this—one way God wants you to experience intimacy with Him is by taking opportunities to pour into the people around you. That's one thing you can do to enjoy deep friendship with God.

Examples from Apostle Paul

Let's think about the life and ministry of the apostle Paul. God inspired him to write much of the Holy Bible. Through His ministry, the gospel was shared in so many places with so many people. In those ways, you could say Paul poured into multiple churches and, in a way, is still pouring into people today.

However, a big part of Paul's ministry was his personal relationships. First, Paul was poured into by a believer named Barnabas. In turn, Paul continued what Barnabas started with him. When we look at his personal relationships, we see him constantly pouring into people like Silas, Timothy, Titus, and the couple, Aquila and Priscilla.

Paul obviously had his eyes fixed on Christ. A natural overflow from that focus was seeing the importance of pouring into individuals amid his broader ministry. Silas, Timothy, Titus, and Aquila and Priscilla were personally strengthened as Paul mentored and poured into them, and this effect extended to their own ministries and faithfulness to Christ.

Silas's experiences with Paul on their missionary journey, Aquila and Priscilla's co-laboring in building and encouraging the church, and Timothy's and Titus's growth as leaders all show us a beautiful picture of biblical mentorship and multiplication. Paul was the apostle to the Gentiles, whose message of the Good News of Christ has now reached millions of people. He was also the tent-making preacher who not only saw individuals but also poured into them from the overflow of what God was pouring into him. The effect was that Paul and those he mentored enjoyed deep friendship with God and continued in their ministries. This, of course, was not the only contributing factor to their deep friendships with God, but it is an important one. Paul not only poured out what God had placed within him to the world, but he also poured it into individual people around him.

> *When you are walking in deep friendship with God, He provides all you need to pour into others.*

You and your church staff can follow this example of pouring into individuals in your church from the overflow of what God is pouring into you as you walk in deep friendship with Him. One exercise a church staff or lay leaders can implement to hold each other accountable for this would be to make a list of the people each staff member is going to pour into over the course of a year. Then, update this list yearly.

Personally, you can keep a list of those you have poured into and who they are pouring into now. When you are walking in deep friendship with God, He provides all you need to pour into others. The more you sincerely pour into others out of His supply, the closer you will find yourself walking in deep friendship with God. It all works together. So, who are you pouring into?

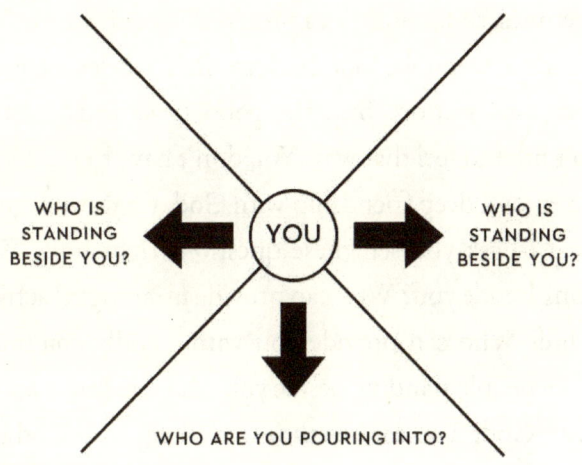

Who Is Standing Beside You?

Question Two: Who is standing beside you? One thing that I (Ken) enjoy doing is coaching youth sports. Several years ago, in the middle of a game, one of my players came to me after a play that didn't go so well on the football field. He told me, "Coach, these boys here, they're trying to hurt my teammates." I looked at him and said, "Well, let's not let that happen. I need you to block and give it your very best." What that player was really saying was, "Hey, I want to stand beside my teammates, and I want my teammates to stand beside me." And guess what? When that happened, he felt the sense of a team that was really important.

For us in ministry, we can often find ourselves feeling lonely. The statistics we shared with you indicate that ministers often go through life, even through their entire careers, feeling like there's nobody standing beside them.

My (Ken) father, who was a minister, told me many times, "Sometimes, son, ministry can feel really, really lonely." That makes sense when we look back to the statistics we listed in the previous section. But, the good news today is that it doesn't have to feel that way. You don't have to feel lonely.

To enjoy a deep friendship with God, we want to encourage you to ask yourself these questions right now. Who is standing beside you? Who can provide meaningful activity in your life? Who can provide you with a godly community? Who are people standing beside you who you know are walking with God? You can see they're walking with God by the way they live their lives in the community and the way they're leading in their families. They are a group of people with whom you can share a Bible verse or a thought. They are people with whom you have life-giving friendships. They are the people who are right there with you, in the trenches.

> *Walking in deep friendship with God means choosing to do life on the right path with each other—together.*

Godly Friendship in Scripture

Scripture is filled with examples of leaders who intentionally surrounded themselves with godly friendship to stand alongside. In David and Jonathan's friendship alone, we see so many lasting benefits of choosing the right people to stand beside. In 1 Samuel 18:1–14, we see friends honoring each other's strengths and promoting one another above themselves. In 1 Samuel 20:41–42, we see friends vulnerably becoming emotional before one another and speaking blessing over each other's lives. In 2 Samuel 1:25–26, we see a friend express how much he needed the other.

When we stand beside godly people, we can talk out with them what has been taught into us. We can grieve with them that which has become broken in us. We can celebrate with them that which has been victorious in us. We can dream together, pray together, imagine the future together, process the past together, laugh hysterically together, and put tension on the right things together.

Walking in deep friendship with God means choosing to do life on the right path with each other—together. These are the people who help us hear and discern the voice of God. They place within each other the courage and accountability to get up and do what God wants us to do.

We see some examples of loyalty and friendships in the Bible. Abraham lived this out by showing us loyalty toward Lot (Genesis 14:14–16). Job modeled for us the gift of presence through adversity with friends (Job 2:11–13). Daniel looked out for his friends, Shadrach, Meshach, and Abednego (Daniel 2:49). Jesus, Mary, Martha, and Lazarus spoke their minds honestly with each other (Luke 10:38, John 11:21–23). Paul, Priscilla, and Aquila introduced each other to even more godly friends (Romans 16:3–4).

What about you? *Over forty percent of pastors suffering burnout "feel lonely and isolated," compared to eighteen percent of pastors who have not considered quitting in the past year.*[49] Establishing and maintaining life-giving relationships can be challenging in ministry. As a church leader, you know that. But, let me ask you this: can you name five people who provide this type of meaningful activity in your life? Name the people you can point to and say, "They provide me with godly community. They provide me with life-giving friendship, and I can talk out things that I'm learning with them." Do you have that? Do you have five people?

The stats tell us that you might not. The truth is that when you are trying your very best to enjoy a deep friendship with God and lead others to have a deep friendship with God, you need at least five people who are standing beside you in this way.

Here are some questions that can help you identify who should be standing beside you:

- Do you enjoy being around that person?
- Is there evidence that they are walking with God? (Fruit of the Spirit)
- Are they actively listening to God and trying to do what He says?
- Can they help you grow and develop into the likeness of Christ, or do they have a history of being in toxic relationships?

After you identify these five people, here are some additional questions that may be helpful:

- Do they know they are on your list?
- Have you scheduled regular times to be with them, either in person or via phone, on your calendar?
- Have you been completely honest with them about your struggles?
- Do they feel like they have permission to tell you the truth, really?

Jesus' disciples were taking on an entirely new ministry. Jesus had poured into them while He was on earth. The Holy Spirit led them once He returned to heaven. But, those disciples also had a strong, believing community between them. They were not alone in their beliefs. If someone was a believer in that environment, which could be downright dangerous for believers, their life showed it and their faith could be trusted. They understood each other's struggles and stood beside one another in fulfilling this amazing call of God.

Christians who fail to have someone standing beside them are more susceptible to moral failures and poor decisions that cost them their lifelong work, witness, reputation, families, and careers.

Unfortunately, this isn't always the case. We've all seen the tragic impact of leaders who have failed to have someone stand beside them, whether it's in politics, entertainment, the church, or even examples in Scripture. Christians who fail to have someone standing beside them are more susceptible to moral failures and poor decisions that cost them their lifelong work, witness, reputation, families, and careers.

Pouring into people without standing beside godly people is an unsustainable pace. Choosing a life rhythm of standing beside godly community is a choice leaders must make. It will never happen by accident.

Dr. Glenn Packiam, who is a pastor, author, and Barna senior fellow, shares in his book *The Resilient Pastor*, "These relationships do not flourish by accident. They require attention and intentionality.... Life is too full of the demands of ministry, the chaos of kids' activities, and the many unpredictable events for us to just hope that meaningful connection will just happen.... Anything worth having is worth pursuing. The chase for deep friendships and intimate relationships is a lifelong quest. But it can begin today. If we really want to last in ministry, if we want to emerge from this as truly and fully human beings, then we must take seriously the human vocation of loving well."[50]

If you want to enjoy deep friendship with God, godly community must be a part of it. It is vital to be in relationship with people who can provide spiritual accountability in your life. People you can laugh hysterically with, people with whom you can talk out the things that have been talked into you. People you can just stand with in the community. That's an awesome thing to have if you're going to walk in deep friendship with God.

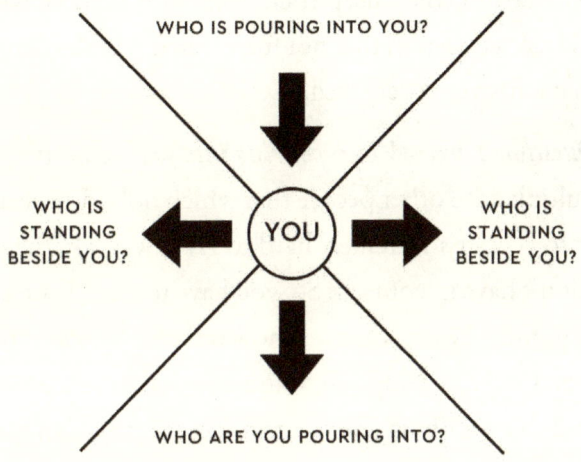

Who Is Pouring Into You?

We've established that pouring into people is a big part of walking in deep friendship with God and enjoying Him every day. But, you and I know that it doesn't matter what you muster up, whether it's your best or worst day. When you get into a rhythm of life where you're pouring out, pouring out, pouring out, and pouring out, eventually your Gatorade jug is going to run dry. Eventually, the water cooler runs dry when it's been poured out, no matter how much support it has.

> *It's extremely hard to give away to others what you don't have in yourself.*

So, that leads to our third question. It's an important one. If you want to enjoy deep friendship with God, maybe you should ask a question that not many leaders in the church today have answered very well.

Question Three: Who is pouring into you? It's very difficult to multiply into other people that which nobody is multiplying into you. It's extremely hard to give away to others what you don't have in yourself. So, you have to ask, "Who's pouring into me?" Now, what we know is that God wants to pour into us. God has things He wants to speak to us, whisper to us, and share with us. He wants to do that through his Holy Spirit, who can help us, teach us, and be a counselor to us. God wants to do that through His word, so it can be a lamp to our feet and a light and to our path. Obviously, God wants to pour into us.

So does Jesus. He says, "I am the vine, you are the branches. He who abides in Me, and I in him, bears much fruit; for without Me you can do nothing" (John 15:5 NKJV). These words of Jesus, like everything He said, are important. In this simple verse, Jesus boils down what life in Him is like: it's abiding. Some translations call it remaining. It means maintaining a deep, growing, and vibrant friendship with God.

The image Jesus uses is of a branch connected to a vine. Apart from that connection, a branch is a stick; it's useless for anything except kindling. But, when that branch is locked into the vine, it finds its life and nutrients flowing into it. Similarly, when we remain in Jesus, we will find our very life found in Him. And, when we are connected to the vine, God's Spirit produces fruit in us, making our hearts reflect the very nature of Christ.

But there are also certain things on the earth that God wants to use as tangible expressions to communicate with us. One thing you could do is ask yourself what you are doing to strategically position yourself to receive what God wants to give you.

Consider this reality: we've already noted that the vast majority of pastors do not have a close friend, confidant, or mentor. Our team sees this often as we meet with pastors across North America. Why is that? Why don't leaders of churches position themselves to be poured into by people who are also walking in deep friendship with God?

Maybe it is because they feel like admitting they need a mentor is the ultimate sign of weakness, although you and I both know the opposite is true. Or, maybe it's the exact opposite end of the spectrum. Maybe the leader feels so sure of himself that he honestly sees no need for a mentor. Maybe the leader would get a mentor, but fears what the mentor might find if given intimate enough access to his life. I'm sure there are many more reasons, but one thing remains true: it takes guts to look at a potential leader in the eye and say, "I need you to pour into me."

We are living in days right now where church leaders sometimes seem like they are dropping like flies. The reasons are many: feeling like a failure, insecurity, exhaustion, addiction, bondage, distraction, isolation, boredom, and so forth. Even many who stay in leadership sometimes come across as walking zombies. And in most cases, there is one common denominator: they lack a mentor who can intentionally pour into them.

We typically assume that mentors are only for the up-and-coming guy or girl or the wannabe leader who has not yet "arrived." Remember Rudy Ruettiger's character in the 1993 classic *Rudy*? It's the story of a young man whose lifelong dream was to play football for the University of Notre Dame. We relate to his story because in certain seasons, we, too, have had to fight and scrap and crawl to get where we were heading.

In re-telling Rudy's story, in his greatest moments of need, he was surrounded by guides—mentors who could pave the way for his wisest next steps. When I close my eyes, I can picture one of his guides, Fortune, in the tunnel right underneath "Touchdown Jesus," giving Rudy an all-time speech. Rudy may have been an unknown wannabe with incredible challenges before him, but his motivation to achieve his goal likely influenced his mentors in their dedication to him.

Every Leader Needs a Mentor

Watching an inspiring movie about someone who had mentors and guidance sounds good, but it doesn't end there. We tend to celebrate those special victorious moments for "lower level" wannabes like Rudy, and we assume that seasoned leaders with high capacity don't have near the need.

But, many significant leaders, often respected and admired, also positioned themselves to be poured into by others.

In the movie, there was a time when Rudy got discouraged. But, he had people pouring into him, so he continued forward. The principle isn't limited to the movies.

Dr. Benjamin Mays, a former president of Morehouse College, mentored Dr. Martin Luther King, Jr., from the time King was an undergraduate student. Mother Teresa, whose name has become synonymous with compassion, humility, and service to the poor, found a mentor in Father Michael van der Peet.[51]

Billy Graham was one of the greatest evangelists the world has ever known. He preached to live audiences of 215 million people in more than 185 countries.[52] The world will never be the same due to his influence. But, did you know that for the last fifteen years of his life, he was still being poured into? Imagine Billy Graham asking you to be that guy! Every Saturday, Pastor Don Wilton drove I-26 from Spartanburg, South Carolina, to Montreat, North Carolina, to pour into a highly effective leader who was wise enough to know he'd always need someone else's counsel and encouragement.[53]

> *Church leaders and all Christians need more than just content to pour into their lives.*

So, here's the question: have you taken time in this season of your life to actually name where you're going to strategically place yourself so you can receive what God wants to do in your life? Maybe there are conferences, webinars, online media, or digital content you have access to. Maybe you are using lots of other things as places to receive the things God wants to give you.

But we want to highlight this last of the three questions because it involves people, not just places, to receive content. As we meet with church leadership, we find that very few church leaders actually have other people who God is using to pour into their lives. You could call these disciple-makers, mentors, coaches, or whatever you like. We ask you, who is the person God is using to pour into your life?

For Ken, it's his mentor, Franklin, who served as a collegiate campus minister for his entire career. He served in several universities, but most of his career was at the University of Georgia. He spent his entire career investing, developing, and teaching college students a biblical worldview. This biblical worldview would prepare them to be godly leaders at work and at home. God used him to prepare thousands of students for the days ahead.

While it has been many years since I (Ken) was in college, Franklin and I have maintained a strong friendship. Franklin continues to invest in my life on a weekly basis. We eat breakfast regularly, and in those times, I know I can bring anything I'm wrestling with to Franklin, who will provide his opinion and advice. I trust Franklin's advice because I know he walks with God.

Franklin is deeply committed to his walk with Christ and it's evident in the way he lives his life. Anytime I have had significant decisions to make regarding family or career, he's held off making those before having a conversation with Franklin. For example, I remember the numerous conversations I had with Franklin before resigning from my job at Lifeway Christian Resources to focus on starting Connect Ministries. He provided continuous spiritual support, and his wisdom played a tremendous role in starting Connect Ministries. I know I can call Franklin at any moment and he'll answer his phone. It's hard to imagine doing life without someone like Franklin walking alongside me.

When a church leader tries to lead a church without having this person pouring into their life, they become spiritually dry. When they're spiritually dry, they have very little to offer to other people. When that happens, a church leader ends up making bad decisions and bad choices because they feel like they're operating on an island in isolation from other people. When a person doesn't have this in their life, they often lack vulnerability, the ability to be transparent and open up to someone else. They don't have anybody that they can go to and say, "I need help." They don't have someone they can go to and say, "Would you teach me?" They don't have anybody they can go to and say, "Could I ask you some questions and you share with me your wisdom, your input, your expertise?"

Church leaders and all Christians need more than just content to pour into their lives. They each need a wise person God can use to be godly counsel into their life so they can make the best decisions moving forward. This is vital for church leaders so they can experience all that God wants to do in their lives so that they can be spiritually healthy and lead a spiritually healthy church that people on the outside would want to join.

We can think about people who have poured into us over the years. It is more than having an older and wiser person meet with you. There are some characteristics for those who can pour into us that make it work:

- They themselves have deep friendship with God. *They pursue the Lord. They have shown significant growth in the Lord.*

- They will consistently show up in your life. You can admire a leader from a distance, but it doesn't count if you just read their books or meet them at a conference. *You need access to this person.*

- This person is willing to talk with you about some of the struggles they are walking through and how they navigate them. *Someone who always presents only the good things in their life is not presenting a very real-life experience.*

- When you are around them, you're challenged to deepen your friendship with God. *They don't stay surface-level with you, but they share authentically about their walk with the Lord.*

- They are willing to listen to what is happening in your life. *They're not always trying to dominate the conversation; they approach it with a very humble spirit.*

You want whoever is pouring into you to be bringing out the best in you, who is bringing out your God-given gifts and helping you realize where you can use them. They are building you up, and that is very empowering.

If you want to enjoy a deep friendship with God, it also involves answering this question: who is pouring into you? To effectively answer this question, you'll have to look at your schedule. Having resources and people pour into you will not happen by accident. You won't coincidentally have resources and people pouring into you. So, it has to show up on your schedule. What are you doing to proactively pursue resources and people to pour into your life so that you have something to offer to the people that you're leading?

> *When you are living out the positive answers to these questions, it's going to send your church insiders out and it's going to bring the outsiders into your church.*

Take Note

So, there you have it. Three simple questions that will help you as you seek deep friendship with God. (1) Who are you pouring into? (2) Who is standing beside you? (3) Who is pouring into you? Sounds pretty easy, doesn't it? But we know how difficult it can be.

As you incorporate these things into your schedule, and as you take these three questions seriously, you'll see a level of friendship with God that you may not have experienced before. And when you are enjoying a deep friendship with God so much that He's just oozing out of you, people are drawn to you, and people want to know what you have. They see it not only in your life but also in those around you and in the life of your church. When you are living out the positive answers to these questions, it will send your church insiders out, and it will bring the outsiders into your church.

That's the type of church that you desire to lead, and that's the type of church your community is looking for as they search for where God might be leading them to get plugged in. Now, it's your turn. Write these three questions on a piece of paper. Then, write real-life names around each one of these questions. If you like, write these questions and related real-life names by different points of the *X* in the diagram above. Don't hurry through it. If you have a question that doesn't have a name by it, that's okay. Write a name in that place and seek out that relationship with someone who will pour into you, or someone who will stand beside you, or someone you will pour into.

Once you've completed that, we challenge you to share it with at least one other person. Sit down and show them, "Look, here is who I am pouring into, here is who's standing beside me, and here is who I'm going to have to pour into me in the days ahead." When you do this, you'll be on your way to being a church that meets new people and engages them into the life of your church.

Take a few minutes and complete the Connect Assessment to gauge your churches effectiveness in Enjoying Deep Friendship with God.

Go to https://www.connect-ministries.com/assessment and enter the code CONNECTEDCHURCH for a free assessment.

CONCLUSION

Think Like a Chef

It's gonna be worth it. Read that again, remind yourself, and reinforce it with your team. It's going to be worth it. But, only if you continue to take the next right step along the way.

It was the great Dale Carnegie who once said, "Knowledge isn't power until it's applied." [54] If you're not careful, you'll quickly move on to the next meeting, book, the subscribed podcast, the newest conference, or the most recently advertised workshop. All those things are great, but what you need most right now is to slow down, process, and walk out what has been taught to you.

It's time to prepare the meal. The tried-and-true recipe has now been passed down to you. So, put on your chef's hat and be faithful stewards of the four ingredients. The wisest leaders have a supernatural knack for continuously taking the next right step along their leadership journey.

If we were in your shoes, there are three wise next steps we would now take.

First, shift your mindset to think like a chef. This will ensure you are thinking about the right things and not unreflectively doing only the most pressing things. In much the same way as a chef envisions the prepared meal, keep your ministry goals in mind. Putting everything together takes time and preparation, just like a gourmet meal.

To cook like a chef, focus on the ingredients and how your team will use them to create remarkable experiences. These ingredients are not to help you create remarkable experiences, but to help your church meet new people. How you think is just as important as what you do. As God uses you to initiate change in the season to come, you'll need to ensure your mindset shifts along the way, too.

It's a powerful force when teams and organizations are courageous enough to shift their mindset. America watched while the New Orleans Saints modeled this right before our very eyes. The 2005 NFL season left their team and their city's morale unimaginably low. With their home city completely ravaged by Hurricane Katrina while also enduring a 3–13 season record, one thing became very clear—something had to change. Their team needed it, but more importantly, all of New Orleans did, too. So, they shifted their mindset. They changed their thinking. The result was one of the most inspirational moments the sports world has ever witnessed.

Under the leadership of head coach Sean Payton and quarterback Drew Brees, the Saints adopted a new mindset that focused on unity, resilience, and the shared goal of bringing joy and pride back to their community. After enduring so much loss, they focused on connecting with their community and providing inspirational leadership. They installed a dynamic offense and became known for winning results on the field and high community engagement off the field. The very next season, they went 10–6 and made it all the way to the NFC Championship Game. Just three years later, they became king of the hill in all of football by winning the Super Bowl. The team's newfound winning mindset mirrored the resilience and determination displayed by the people of New Orleans in the face of adversity, and it remains one of the most iconic stories in the history of the NFL.

> *Way before you win, you must learn to think like a winner.*

Their challenges are different from yours, and yours are different from ours. What's most important is how we decide to respond to the circumstances right in front of us. So, just think. Think about it. Think about what it's going to be like to chase the future God has in store for your church.

Stay disciplined to ask yourself and your team the right questions. Doing so is going to spark brand new ideas and innovation. Remain a curious learner and watch God open up doors for non-stop learning and growth. Imagine the lives that will be impacted along the way. Fill your mind with God-sized courage for what needs to be changed and empower the leaders around you to take their part. Stay tender and empathetic for real life people and keep thinking strategically about how to meet them.

It's a mindset and a process. It's bigger than a list of to-dos. And it takes laser-beam, disciplined thinking over extended periods of time. Way before you win, you must learn to think like a winner. When you do, just think about all God will do around you.

Second, cook with the right amount of all four ingredients all the time. Your favorite meals, entrees and desserts were made in that exact same way. No ingredient is more important than the other—they all matter all the time, and you now know what they are:

1. *Create remarkable experiences.* They come in all shapes and sizes and can cost a lot or a little. We all crave them, whether large or small. It's all about how people feel after the moment.

2. *Build life-giving relationships.* The people you're trying to reach long to belong, and they will eventually choose the group who most intentionally welcomes them in and adds value to their lives.

3. *Execute a clear plan.* Passion alone won't carry you all the way to your desired future, but passion paired with a well-executed, comprehensive strategy can get you there.

4. *Enjoy deep friendship with God.* There's a major difference between working for God and walking with Him. Abba desires ongoing intimacy with

you and those you lead. You can't fake the marinade.

Finally, create the space and time you need to rightly cook the meal in the way it is intended to be made. That starts with being strategic and proactive in organizing the time spent on your calendar. You are going to need time to plan, think, brainstorm, listen, create, and collaborate. You need strategic time and space on your calendar to align your team, train and equip the leaders around you, evaluate effectiveness, and make the necessary tweaks and changes along the way. If your calendar does not reflect your priority of cooking with these four ingredients, the meal you long to serve people will likely miss the mark.

Connect Ministries is eager and available to help you with this. That's why we created Connect Coaching, a resource designed to share our extensive learnings from helping over two thousand churches meet over 250,000 new people since 2006. We work with pastors all over the country, many of whom are discouraged and frustrated because they are struggling to meet new people. Their churches are not growing, and after much exhaustion, they honestly don't know what to do next. Connect Coaching helps your church develop a clear plan to meet new people.

This typically begins with an assessment tool that helps you and your team gauge your current effectiveness in each of the four ingredients. Based on the thorough results of the Connect Assessment, our team works one on one with your church in a coaching environment, either online or in person.

To learn more, go to our website, connect-ministries.com, and take the free quiz. It's a free, four-question, two-minute quiz that will give you our personalized recommendations on how to take the first step toward being the kind of church that effectively meets new people.

How does this assessment work in a practical setting? Recently, I worked with one of our churches in Alabama, which participates in the Connect Coaching program. This particular church is not located in a big city, so they are not surrounded by thousands and thousands of people. In fact, if you were to have driven by this church twenty years ago, you would probably not even notice it. It was a much smaller church than it is today.

However, they developed a strategy, and they began to work that strategy. As part of that strategy, they knew the importance of having a culture where people would encounter the gospel and then assimilate into a small group where they would have a sense of belonging.

Recently, I (Ken) was reviewing the results from the Connect 360 Assessment my church had completed. Their scores as a whole were consistently above average. I found it so encouraging to see a church that was growing and implementing a strategy. Now, this church averages well over 1,500 people on campus each Sunday. But, there was one score that caught my attention. They scored 4.48 out of 5.0 in the area that rates "deep friendship with God." Do you think the fact that their church has a culture where "deep friendship with God" is modeled and taught had anything to do with their church growth?

Not only did they score high in "deep friendship with God," but their overall combined score was above 4.2. In this case, there is a direct correlation between a church that scores high on all four ingredients and church growth. It is very hard to have accidental church growth. This church has been very intentional and is working with a great strategy.

I called their executive pastor and asked what he thought contributed to such high scores related to "deep friendship with God"—what are they doing to get these high scores? "First, our church has responded extremely well to the Great Commission mandate, and we have been incredibly blessed to provide opportunities. This is not the only one but it has been a major shift in the lives of our people in our community through experiencing short-term missions. . . . Second, we offer multiple opportunities for discipleship at all levels of growth or lack of. Providing opportunities that meet people where they are has been monumental. Lastly, I would say pushing ways to serve in the life of the church gives people the opportunity to truly own their faith and be a part of the church."

You're right on the brink of a breakthrough, so keep taking the wisest next step you know to take. Your team is about to become even more aligned; your church is about to become more united; diverse backgrounds and brains are about to collaborate; and long-standing problems are going to be met with highly effective solutions. People who once felt bored, aimless, and without direction will be filled with passion and zeal about the purpose and opportunity they've now discovered at your church.

The lost are going to be found, and the found are going to be grown up. Things are about to change. It's going to be worth it!

About the Authors

DR. KEN THOMAS
PRESIDENT OF CONNECT MINISTRIES

Ken graduated from the University of Georgia with a Bachelor of Science in education. He also received a Master of Divinity degree from Southwestern Theological Seminary and earned his doctorate in education from the Southern Baptist Theological Seminary. Today, he combines his great education with his passion for teaching, equipping, and leading to help churches meet new people. He began his work in camp ministry in 1989 as a summer staffer (Ridgecrest Conference Center) and has served in various capacities over the years. He served for over nine years at Lifeway Christian Resources (Nashville, Tennessee) on the Student Events Team where he was instrumental in starting a children's camp called Centri-Kid. He also served as Senior Director of WinShape Camps, as he served with a great team the camps grew from 1,800 campers to over 40,000 campers during his time of leadership.

Ken has served in many different capacities over years alongside his full-time work in ministry. He served as an elected official (Alderman) in the town of Nolensville, Tennessee, he has served as the volunteer Chaplain for the University of Texas at Arlington baseball team, the volunteer Chaplain for Belmont University Baseball Team, a founding member of the board for Rolling Hills Community Church, a member of the Touchdown Club board for the Oconee County Football team, and in various other leadership roles in the community.

Ken now serves as President of Connect Ministries which helps churches connect with their community and meet new people. He and Gabe Norris started Connect Ministries in 2006, and God has used this ministry to partner with over three thousand churches and has impacted over 500,000 people with the message of Jesus Christ. Connect Ministries has created and launched several resources including Connect Camps, Connect Coaching, Connect Conference, Connect FCA Camp and the Connect Residency.

He has taught small groups in his local church for over twenty-five years and enjoys preaching and speaking at churches, providing coaching for leaders and churches, and speaking at conferences throughout the United States. He and his wife, Norma, have been married for over thirty years and have three children. Learn more at www.connect-ministries.com.

GABE NORRIS
VICE PRESIDENT OF CONNECT MINISTRIES

Gabe graduated from the University of Georgia's Terry College of Business and Beeson Divinity School at Samford University. He began his work in camp ministry in 1997 as a YMCA counselor and went on to serve in leadership roles with Student Life for Kids Camps and Lifeway's Crosspoint and Centri-Kid Camps, and later as Director of WinShape Camps for Communities. During his twelve years of leadership, WinShape Camps for Communities' geographical reach expanded by 330 percent and annual camper totals grew by more than 930 percent. He also helped launch Connect Day Camps and has been instrumental in expanding Connect Ministries across North America and into other countries, equipping churches and leaders to engage their communities.

Over the last twenty-five years, Gabe has preached and taught to audiences of all ages, including children, teenagers, college students, and leaders in churches and the marketplace, across the U. S. and internationally. He has trained hundreds of communicators and equipped thousands of young adults to discover their strengths, pursue their calling, and make a meaningful impact in their communities. Known for his encouragement, passion, and investment in emerging leaders, he has also coached youth sports and led weekly small group Bible studies for more than two decades.

Gabe now serves as Vice President of Connect Ministries, which he co-founded with Ken Thomas in 2006. The ministry has partnered with more than 2,500 churches and impacted over 500,000 people with the message of Jesus Christ. Gabe oversees Connect's marketing, creative, and staff teams and played a key role in forming a strategic alliance with the Fellowship of Christian Athletes. He has helped launch resources including Connect Camps, Connect Coaching, Connect Conference, Connect Marketing, Connect FCA Camps, and the Connect Residency. Under his leadership, Connect has grown to become a trusted partner for churches seeking to engage their communities and connect with new people.

He and his wife, Allyson, have been married for twenty-five years and live in Bishop, Georgia, with their three daughters—Neely, Ansley Jane, and Audrey. Learn more at www.connect-ministries.com.

REFERENCES

Notes

[1] Hayes, Adam. "Word-of-Mouth Marketing: Meaning and Uses in Business." Investopedia. July 2, 2024. https://www.investopedia.com/terms/w/word-of-mouth-marketing.asp.

[2] "Help Your Visitors Connect, Engage, and Feel Like They Belong." Church Community Builder. Church management software. https://churchcommunitybuilder.com.

[3] Pravin, Pranjal. "Ritz-Carlton Business Strategy: Maximum Customer Satisfaction." The Strategy Story. June 9, 2021. https://thestrategystory.com/2021/06/09/ritz-carlton-business-strategy.

[4] Heath, Chip, and Dan Heath. *The Power of Moments: Why Certain Moments Have Extraordinary Impact*. Transworld, 2017.

[5] Bair, Dave, and Steve Caton. *The Assimilation Engine: Four Processes That Drive How People Connect to Your Church.* Church Community Builder, 2013. https://tcsba.com/hp_wordpress/wp-content/uploads/2018/12/ebook-assimilationengine.pdf.

[6] Godin, Seth. *Purple Cow: Transform Your Business by Being Remarkable.* Portfolio, 2003.

[7] Soderbergh, Steven, dir. *Moneyball.* Columbia Pictures, 2011.

[8] Toyota Blog. "Andon—Toyota Production System Guide." May 31, 2016. https://mag.toyota.co.uk/andon-toyota-production-system.

[9] Smietana, Bob. "YouVersion Bible App Hires Former Facebook Exec to Fuel Growth." Religion News Service. January 19, 2023. https://religionnews.com/2023/01/19/youversion-bible-app-hires-former-facebook-exec-to-fuel-growth.

"About YouVersion." YouVersion. https://www.youversion.com/mission.

[10] Bower, Tracy. "Missing Your People." Forbes. January 10, 2021. Updated January 12, 2022. https://www.forbes.com/sites/tracybrower/2021/01/10/missing-your-people-why-belonging-is-so-important-and-how-to-create-it.

[11] Bower, "Missing Your People."

[12] Bower, "Missing Your People."

¹³ Choi, Karmel W., et al.. *American Journal of Psychiatry* 177, no. 10 (2020). https://psychiatryonline.org/doi/10.1176/appi.ajp.2020.19111158.

¹⁴ Holt-Lunstad, Julianne, Timothy B. Smith, and J. Bradley Layton. "Social Relationships and Mortality Risk: A Meta-analytic Review." *PLOS Medicine* 7, no. 7 (2010). https://journals.plos.org/plosmedicine/article?id=10.1371/journal.pmed.1000316.

Steptoe, Andrew, Aparna Shankar, Panayotes Demakakos, and Jane Wardle. "Social Isolation, Loneliness, and All-Cause Mortality in Older Men and Women." *PNAS* 110, no. 15 (2013). https://doi.org/10.1073/pnas.1219686110.

¹⁵ Office of the Surgeon General. "Our Epidemic of Loneliness and Isolation: The U.S. Surgeon General's Advisory on the Healing Effects of Social Connection and Community." U. S. Department of Health and Human Services, 2023.

¹⁶ Pezirkianidis, Christos, Evangelia Galanaki, Georgia Raftapoulou, Despina Moraitou, and Anastassios Stalikas. "Adult Friendship and Wellbeing: A Systematic Review with Practical Implications." *Frontiers in Psychology* 14 (2023). https://doi.org/10.3389/fpsyg.2023.1059057.

Blieszner, Rosemary, Aaron M. Ogletree, and Rebecca G. Adams. "Friendship in Later Life: A Research Agenda." *Innovation in Aging* 3, no. 1 (2019). https://doi.org/10.1093/geroni/igz005.

[17] Holt-Lunstad, Smith, and Layton, "Social Relationships and Mortality Risk."

[18] Cox, Daniel A. "The State of American Friendship: Change, Challenges, and Loss." Survey Center on American Life. June 8, 2021. https://www.americansurveycenter.org/research/the-state-of-american-friendship-change-challenges-and-loss.

[19] Kannan, Viji Diane, and Peter J. Veazie. "US Trends in Social Isolation, Social Engagement, and Companionship—Nationally and by Age, Sex, Race/Ethnicity, Family Income, and Work Hours, 2003–2020." *SSM–Population Health* 21 (2023). https://doi.org/10.1016/j.ssmph.2022.101331.

[20] Twenge, Jean M., Jonathan Haidt, Andrew B. Blake, Cooper McAllister, Hannah Lemon, and Astrid Le Roy. *Journal of Adolescence* 93, no. 1 (2021). https://doi.org/10.1016/j.adolescence.2021.06.006.

[21] Lukert, Luke. "Feelings of Seclusion and Not Belonging Plague Americans." WTOP News. July 12, 2023. https://wtop.com/health-fitness/2023/07/feelings-of-seclusion-and-not-belonging-plague-americans.

[22] Abrams, Zara. "The Science of Why Friendships Keep Us Healthy." *Monitor on Psychology* 54, no. 4 (2023). https://www.apa.org/monitor/2023/06/cover-story-science-friendship.

Ewing, Lexi, Chloe A. Hamza, Kaylea Walsh, Abby L. Goldstein, and Nancy L. Heath. "A Qualitative Investigation of the Positive and Negative Impacts of the COVID-19

Pandemic on Post-secondary Students' Mental Health and Well-being." *Emerging Adulthood* 10, no. 5, 2022. https://doi.org/10.1177/21676968221121590.

[23] Nieuwhof, Carey. "12 Disruptive Church Trends That Will Rule 2022 (and the Post-pandemic Era)." Carey Nieuwhof (website). https://careynieuwhof.com/12-disruptive-church-trends-that-will-rule-2022-and-the-post-pandemic-era.

[24] Holcomb, Drew. "Find Your People." Track 2 on *Strangers No More*. Magnolia, 2023.

[25] Roberts, Amy. "Tailgating by the Numbers." CNN. September 1, 2016. https://www.cnn.com/2015/11/25/living/tailgating-by-the-numbers/index.html.

[26] Rotary International. My Rotary (web portal). https://my.rotary.org/en/membership-dues.

[27] Pow, Alec. "Country Club Membership Costs—What Fees Do Clubs Charge?" ThePricer. https://www.thepricer.org/country-club-membership-cost.

[28] Bair and Caton, *The Assimilation Engine*.

[29] Bair and Caton, *The Assimilation Engine*.

[30] Kibitzor. "Trader Joe's Did Something Awesome." Reddit.com. 2009. https://www.reddit.com/r/reddit.com/comments/agsb4/trader_joes_did_something_awesome.

[31] Hartnett, Kelley. "By the Numbers: Guests, Attendance, and the Back Door." Church Marketing Sucks. October 7,

2015. http://churchmarketingsucks.com/2015/10/by-the-numbers-guests-attendance-and-the-back-door.

[32] Mandrell, Ben. *The Power of Personal: Building Stronger Connections in a Lonely World*. Lifeway Research, 2023.

[33] Bahr, Candace, and Ginita Wall. "What Ben Franklin Can Teach You About the Power of Compound Interest." Women's Insitute for Financial Education. https://www.wife.org/a-penny-saved.htm.

See also:

Meyer, Michael. *Benjamin Franklin's Last Bet*. Mariner, 2022.

[34] Sugarman, Jay. "Invest Like a Genius: The Investment Secret of Benjamin Franklin, Albert Einstein, and Warren Buffett." Safehold. September 27, 2021. https://www.safeholdinc.com/invest-like-a-genius-the-investment-secret-of-benjamin-franklin-albert-einstein-and-warren-buffett/#:~:text=Franklin%20described%20compound%20interest%20this,has%20to%20make%20more%20money.

[35] "At What Mile Do Most Runners Quit a Marathon?" Running State. https://runningstate.com/at-what-mile-do-most-runners-quit-a-marathon.

[36] Segal, Troy. "Enron Scandal and Accounting Fraud: What Happened?" Investopedia. Updated December 3, 2024. https://www.investopedia.com/updates/enron-scandal-summary.

See also:

U. S. Congress Joint Committee on Taxation. *Report of Investigation of Enron Corporation and Related Entities Regarding Federal Tax and Compensation Issues, and Policy Recommendations*. PDF. 2003, p. 77, 84.

[37] Compassion International. "About Us: Compassion International History." https://www.compassion.com/history.htm.

[38] Blackaby, Henry, and Richard Blackaby. *Spiritual Leadership: Moving People on to God's Agenda*. B&H, 2001.

[39] Doran, George T. "There's a S.M.A.R.T. Way to Write Management's Goals and Objectives." *Management Review* 70, no. 11 (1981): p. 35–36.

[40] Blackaby, Henry T., and Claude V. King. *Experiencing God: Knowing and Doing the Will of God*. B&H, 2008, p. 209.

[41] Pastoral Care Inc. "Statistics in the Ministry: Newly Revised Statistics." https://www.pastoralcareinc.com/statistics.

This statistic is based on research conducted before the COVID-19 pandemic.

The statistics from Pastoral Care Inc. are based on research from Fuller Institute of Church Growth, George Barna, Lifeway Research, Schaeffer Institute of Leadership Development, Christianity Today, and Pastoral Care Inc.

[42] Rainer, Sam. "4 Reasons Pastors Lack Work–Life Balance." BP Toolbox. January 8, 2024. https://www.baptistpress.com/resource-library/bptoolbox/4-reasons-pastors-lack-work-life-balance.

[43] Focus on the Family. *Pastoral Ministries 2009 Survey*. PDF. p. 9. https://www.parsonage.org/images/pdf/2009PMSurvey.pdf.

[44] Pastoral Care Inc. "Statistics in the Ministry."

The statistics from Pastoral Care Inc. are based on research from Fuller Institute of Church Growth, George Barna, Lifeway Research, Schaeffer Institute of Leadership Development, Christianity Today, and Pastoral Care Inc.

[45] Pastoral Care Inc. "Statistics in the Ministry."

(See source note 45.)

[46] Pastoral Care Inc. "Statistics in the Ministry."

(See previous source note 45.)

[47] Pastoral Care, Inc. "Clarification and Discussion Concerning Our Statistics." https://www.pastoralcareinc.com/statistics/clarification-on-statistics.

This source notes that the higher statistic cited is over twenty years old. Varying survey methods and tools (like using the term *pastor* versus *minister*) may account for the wide range of available statistics.

[48] Fast Company Executive Board. "You Get the Greatest Returns When You Invest in People." Fast Company.

August 2, 2022. https://www.fastcompany.com/90772379/you-get-the-greatest-returns-when-you-invest-in-people

[49] Barna Group. "Pastors Share Top Reasons They've Considered Quitting in the Past Year." Barna (website). April 27, 2022. https://www.barna.com/research/pastors-quitting-ministry.

[50] Packiam, Glenn. *The Resilient Pastor: Leading Your Church in a Rapidly Changing World*. Baker, 2022.

[51] Merrill, Jennifer. "Top 25 Mentoring Relationships in History." The Chronicle of Evidence-based Mentoring. https://www.evidencebasedmentoring.org/top-25-mentoring-relationships-in-history.

[52] Lifeway Research. "Billy Graham's Life and Ministry by the Numbers." February 21, 2018. https://research.lifeway.com/2018/02/21/billy-grahams-life-ministry-by-the-numbers.

[53] Flynn, Meredith. "Wilton Reflects on Friendship with Billy Graham." The Baptist Paper. July 10, 2023. https://thebaptistpaper.org/wilton-reflects-on-friendship-with-billy-graham.

[54] Carnegie, Dale. *How to Stop Worrying and Start Living*. Diamond Pocket Books, 2016, p. 92.

www.ingramcontent.com/pod-product-compliance
Lightning Source LLC
Chambersburg PA
CBHW022104090426
42743CB00008B/707